The Royal Pardon

The Royal Pardon is a play filled with action, music and gaiety, specifically intended for informal performance. A company of strolling players, hounded out of a country village by a zealous police constable, are joined by a vagrant soldier, also on the run, who acts as stage manager. When the company is selected by the King of England to perform at the French court their performance is almost sabotaged by the jealous French actors and the constable, who is still on their tail. But the soldier gives such a brilliant performance that the English company wins the French King's prize, while the constable is turned to stone.

This play reflects the authors' interest in drama as something for the community rather than for a limited metropolitan audience. There are different things in it for different members of the audience. It is about order and anarchy, about illusion and reality. It is a plea for an unfettered, vital drama. It is also a vivid piece of theatre for children to watch and to perform.

'Both play and production implicitly question a whole list of the guff that surrounds a tired British theatre, especially the myth that to be serious you have to be pompous and intense.'

Flourish

The Royal Pardon

or
The Soldier who Became
an Actor

JOHN ARDEN
&
MARGARETTA D'ARCY

LONDON
METHUEN & CO LTD
11 NEW FETTER LANE EC4

First published 1967 by Methuen & Co Ltd
Reprinted 1970
Reprinted 1974 by Eyre Methuen Ltd, 11 New Fetter Lane,
London EC4P 4EE
© *1967 by John Arden and Margaretta D'Arcy*
All rights reserved
Printed Offset Litho in Great Britain by
Cox & Wyman Ltd
Fakenham, Norfolk
ISBN 0 413 33410 4

This play is dedicated to
the memory of
GEORGE DEVINE

Authors' Note

This play had its origin in a series of bedtime stories told to our own children (aged 2–6): but we intended the dramatized version to be for a somewhat older age-group. The production in Devon, however, seemed to suggest that there is sufficient in the plot and action to interest even little children, provided it is acted with conviction and with a proper sense of communication between performers and audience. In the Beaford Arts Centre (which is a converted dwelling house) we had an old billiard room, 20 ft by 30 ft, with no raised stage, two doors which were used by the spectators as well as the cast, and an audience of about ninety, who sat very tightly together in an area equivalent to approximately half the room. Along one wall of the room we hung a painted backcloth, but there could clearly be no attempt at illusion, and the smallest children sat on the floor among the feet of the actors. These conditions were not a handicap to be overcome, as we had hoped and indeed planned for them from the beginning. *The Royal Pardon* was never intended as a piece for the regular theatre, although in a theatre with an open stage or even with a small forestage, the play could no doubt be successfully performed. On an ordinary proscenium stage the dialogue might seem long-drawn-out and the action inconsequential, and children might be bored. They weren't, at Beaford. We also used music throughout the play, mostly percussion, made by two players in a sort of cage against one wall of the room. This music accompanied many of the speeches and most of the physical movement. There is no score of it, as it was improvised during rehearsals and gradually fixed into a final form shortly before the play opened. The treatment of costumes was similar. There was no overall design for the production, but each member of the cast was supplied with a dress that seemed appropriate to the character, parts of it being specially made, but combined with garments and accessories which were already in the possession of the actor, or were otherwise borrowed or found. The result of this was to present an apparently logical arrangement of costume that yet could be assigned to no particular period of history. Most of the male members of the company, for instance, wore their own trousers and shoes, and relied upon their coats, hats, and wigs to supply the required indication of character or type. Mr Croke's actors wore masks for their roles in the various 'plays within the play'. But we do not want to appear to be laying down rules for the presentation of *The Royal Pardon*. It is a comedy that we imagine can be produced in many different ways, all of them right. We did not take pains to remove from the text any illusions or psychological nuances which might be above the heads of children. In our experience children prefer to be occasionally puzzled by the behaviour of adults in plays, as this bears out their observations of life outside the theatre.

January 1967   J. A. and M.D'A.

The Royal Pardon

or

The Soldier who Became an Actor

The Royal Pardon was first performed at the Beaford Arts Centre, Devon, on 1 September 1966, under the direction of the authors, with the following cast:

LUKE (A Soldier)	Roger Davenport
Strolling Actors	
THE CLOWN	Nigel Gregory
ESMERALDA	Martha Gibson
MR CROKE	Philip Sayer
MRS CROKE	Maureen Lipman
WILLIAM	Timothy Craven
Villagers	
THE CONSTABLE	John Arden
THE UNDER-CONSTABLE	Frank Challenger
MRS HIGGINBOTTOM (His Wife)	Lesley Joseph
The English Court	
LORD CHAMBERLAIN	Frank Challenger
THE KING	Tamara Hinchco
THE PRINCE	Mark Wing-Davey
The French Court	
AN OFFICER	Nigel Gregory
AN ACTRESS	Lesley Joseph
AN ACTOR	Frank Challenger
THE KING	Rupert Haverbrook
THE PRINCESS	Tamara Hinchco
A COOK	Nigel Gregory

Stage Managed by Valerie Beer
Music composed and played by Boris Howarth and
Russell Howarth
Décor and costumes by Margaret Hogg and Sanny Yen
The action of the play is set in England and France
The period is legendary rather than historical

Act One

The Actors' stage is already set up. It is little more than a small curtained booth with bunting and other cheap decorations. The ACTORS *are heard singing behind it.*

SONG.
      Sun and moon and stars and rainbow
      Drum and trumpet, tambourine,
      A greedy king or a haughty beggar
      A virgin slut or a painted queen –
      Put your boots on, mask your faces
      Heave your cloaks and swing your swords,
      Laugh and weep and stamp with anger,
      Kick your jigs and strut the boards,
      All is painted, all is cardboard
      Set it up and fly it away
      The truest word is the greatest falsehood,
      Yet all is true and all in play –
      Sun and moon and stars and rainbow
      Drum and trumpet, tambourine.

The CLOWN *enters, followed by the '*DRAGON*' [*ESMERALDA*], who nips and worries him as he addresses the audience.*

CLOWN. Ladies and gentlemen, ladies and gentlemen, ladies gentlemen – get-aht-of-it, you've split me breeches –
(*He removes his loose trousers which the* DRAGON *has torn, revealing another pair underneath.*)
Keep him off me, keep him off me – he'll stop the show before we've started – get-aht-of-it, get in – (*He drives the* DRAGON *behind the curtains.*)
Puts you off, dunnit?

Why, I was going to give you a prologue . . . oh yes, here
we are . . .

> Our little play this afternoon,
> Not too early, not too soon,
> Is the glorious story of bold St George
> And how he choked the Dragon's gorge . . .

He didn't hear that, did he? He don't know what's in store
for him, does he? It's all right, it's all clear . . . I'm safe
for a few minutes more . . .

> In days of old this Dragon roamed the land,
> Not one man brave enough against him for to stand.
> The King and all his People were in fear
> For every day the Dragon would appear
> Consuming all in horrible flaming fire.

(*Enter* 'KING' [MR CROKE] *and* 'PRINCESS' [MRS CROKE].)

> Here is the King, here is his lovely Daughter,
> And here's the brutal monster, tearing a'ter –

The DRAGON *comes in again and chases them all off and
round about the stage. After a while the* KING *and* PRINCESS
are left alone.

KING.

> My child, I have spoken to many wise men
> Both north, east, west and south:
> And only one answer have they given to me
> How to stop the Dragon's mouth.
> They say that I must sacrifice to him
> Whatever I hold most dear:
> And that, my dear, I sorely fear,
> Is you, it doth appear.

PRINCESS.

> Oh father, such a horrid fate
> I did not dream nor contemplate.

KING.

> Weep not, faint not, the dragon is so quick

He'll gobble you up in half a tick.

I doubt very much if you'll feel any pain.

PRINCESS.

But father, I shall never see you again.

KING.

Which is so sad indeed, I know not what to say.

But here I must tie you up till the dragon should pass
    this way. (*He binds her.*)

My child, it is for your country and your King

That you must suffer this abominable thing.

There we are, safe and sound . . .

I hear his footsteps beat and pound!

KING   } *together*
PRINCESS

Oh { daughter / father } such a horrid fate,

I did not dream nor contemplate.

Exit KING.

Enter 'ST GEORGE' [WILLIAM].

ST GEORGE.

Why, what is here, as though for sale displayed?

Tied like a parcel, a beautiful young maid?

Speak if you can! She weeps, she cannot utter.

Enter CLOWN.

CLOWN.

Watch out, he's on his way, I see his head!

He's coming for his slice of bread.

Do you want to be the butter?

ST GEORGE.

Who, what, where, when, how?

Do you talk of a dinner or a feast?

CLOWN.

I'm talking of the dreadful scaly beast

Who'll eat you up, lungs, liver, lights and gall!

ST GEORGE.

Aha! I am St George and dragons I appal.

Enter DRAGON.

DRAGON.

A lovely girl, a strong young handsome boy:
Which of the two shall I the best enjoy?

ST GEORGE.

Fight for your life!

DRAGON.

Struggle and strife,
I fight for my dinner!

ST GEORGE.

I fight for my wife!

He kills the DRAGON *after a good deal of business.*
The KING *enters and cheers.*

KING.

Did I hear you say 'wife'?
First we shall have to see whether you suit her social
status.

CLOWN.

Another couple of minutes and this creature would
have ate us –
Such consequential fortitude
Deserves a bit of gratitude.
Go on then, let them wed,
Get the blankets on the bed

KING.

That's quite enough of that –*

* This line is spoken 'out of character' – i.e. CROKE is rebuking an irregular gag by the CLOWN and raises his mask briefly for the purpose.

Sir, you are so brave and glorious,
So splendidly victorious,
That if you want her, you must have her.
Of course, I do suppose I'll have to ask her mother.
Yet am I not the King?
So, with the greatest pleasure,
I render you my treasure.

PRINCESS.

This is too much.
Oh father dear, I never thought –

KING.

Ah not at all,
I expected something of the sort –

CLOWN.

Take her by the hand
Kiss her on the cheek
And you shall have a lovely honeymoon
That'll last you all next week –

(*As he jumps around he steps near the supposedly dead* DRAGON, *who nips him in the rear. His trousers split again revealing yet another pair on underneath.*)

Ow, I've split me breeches, look, they've gone again, I thought you told me he was dead –

The CONSTABLE *comes forward out of the audience.*

CONSTABLE. Right, that'll do. That is the second occasion in this deplorable performance that vulgar and indecent behaviour has taken place. I've got it down in me notebook, it is incontrovertible. Twice, no less, was breeches mentioned and each time they was removed: to the scandal of the populace. Whatever you might get away with in London, we do *not* allow that sort of thing round here. Close your show at once and take yourselves out of this town.

The ACTORS, *crestfallen, remove their masks.*

CROKE. And who, sir, do you think you are? Choosing to address me with such, er, with such, er . . . er, h'm . . .

CONSTABLE. I'm the Constable, that's who. We had a warning about this performance, I may tell you, and my worst fears have been justified. Why – children might have been present. Sickening, I call it. Go on, get out of here before I run you in. Rogues, vagabonds, dirty-minded hooligans.

Enter LUKE.

LUKE (*addressing the audience, while the* ACTORS *sadly pack up their gear*). I wouldn't go quite so far as that meself – dirty-minded, to my mind, is piling it on a bit strong. But they are a slovenly baggagey lot and if they'd been let continue long enough to pass around a hat, they'd ha' got nowt from me in it, I can tell you that plainly. Tearing his pants off – *twice*! Well, did anybody laugh at it – did you? *I* didn't. And what about St George? There was a man, if they'd had the intelligence, to look out a proper play about him, there was a man that could *call* himself a man.

> His sword was strong, his heart was clear;
> Inside his stomach he knew the claws of fear.
> But he fought them first and then he fought again
> The claws of the dragon and the fire and the raving
>   pain,
> And he brought it through to a finish
> And he took the lady by the hand
> And he said 'How dare they offer so frail a sacrifice on
>   this strand?
> The King himself should ha' stood here to defend his
>   ravaged land.
> Coward that he was he must now defend it from me:
> The dragon being dead and his daughter being free,
> I take my stand and I stake my claim.
> Fight me,' declares St George, 'Or forever bear the
>   the blame

That you've lost your crown and your daughter
And your old respected name.'
And so he should ha' fought him and St George should ha'
won, and your useless King done-for, and then you'd have
had a play and a marriage worth celebrating – but as for all
this, it's just rubbish and insulting – I haven't got patience.
Go on, Constable, get rid of 'em, there's no two ways.

CONSTABLE. Ho, indeed, is that so? I'll attend to *you* in a
moment . . .

(*To the* ACTORS.) Come on then, aren't you ready yet? Now
I'm giving you just two more minutes and if you're not on
the move by then –

WILLIAM. Oh be quiet and leave us alone, you dreary little
jack-in-office!

CONSTABLE. What did you say?

WILLIAM. I said –

CONSTABLE. I heard what you said. Abusive language I heard,
to an officer of the law in pursuance of his duty!

(*He blows his whistle. Enter* UNDER-CONSTABLE.)

Ah there you are, Higginbottom. And not before time. Is
this what you call being upon instant readiness in the service
of public order?

UNDER-CONSTABLE. I'm sorry, Mr Hopkins, but my good
wife was just on the process of pitching up a statch, I mean
statching up a pitch, I mean, well, she's yet at it – I mean she
can't discern the eye.

CONSTABLE (*notices his bare legs*). What eye? Your –

UNDER-CONSTABLE (*who is in his underpants*). Trousers. It's
what I'm telling you. She's trying to get the thread into the
needle at this identical moment, but being as you know a
little bit dim-sighted – there you are, you see, look at her.

Enter MRS HIGGINBOTTOM, *trying to thread a needle.*

CONSTABLE. Higginbottom, you are a-casting upon me
mockery and confusion in the very presence of these male-

factors. Just look at 'em there – laughing! You can run this fellar in. Put the cuffs upon him – sharp!

(WILLIAM, *who is laughing the loudest, is suddenly handcuffed by the* UNDER-CONSTABLE.)

Now then, anybody else require any persuading? Or do you do what I tell you and get that clobber on the road!

CROKE. Yes, Officer, just so – no more trouble. We're all going quietly. Hurry up, my dears, don't waste any time. We're not wanted here so we might as well be off.

ESMERALDA. But what about poor William?

WILLIAM. Hey, yes indeed – what about me?

CROKE. My dear William, you *were* rude. You were very rude to the Officer. Most injudicious, my dear boy. There's nothing we can do, you know. We can't *all* be arrested. Well, can we? Good lord, can we?

ESMERALDA. Yes, of course we can, why not?

MRS CROKE. Why not? Why, of course not – we have a responsibility to our public, Esmeralda, which we cannot discharge from prison. Do not be ridiculous, my dear, I beg you – this is no time for foolish jokes.

ESMERALDA.

A foolish joke
To Mrs Croke
Is altogether foolish
And true, when all is said and done
It gets quite hard to see the fun
Of being set upon the run
By all the cops in every town
From Bude to Ballachulish.

(*She sings, with tambourine. The* CLOWN *joins in, and the* ACTORS *all file out, lugging their dismantled gear.*)

Close the show, we're a lousy lot of layabouts,
Close the show, we're obstructing in the street,
Our jokes are blue, our noses too,
Our cash is few, we've stinking feet –

Keep your kids away from danger
Keep your wives away from vice
Never let your husband talk to an actress
For what she does is not quite nice . . .

MRS CROKE. Esmeralda, will you *please* help me to carry this hamper and try not to make worse what was bad before already!

ESMERALDA (*resignedly lifting the load and staggering out with a swirl of her tambourine*). Oh, unjust expulsion, and unprovoked peregrination – I come, I come, reluctantly, I come . . .

CONSTABLE (*once they have all gone*). I will considerately take no action upon that last impertinence, but it's written down, you know – they're noted, in the book!

LUKE. I've just been reading a different book – in Flanders – broken bones and rotted limbs, puddles of blood, a chopped-off skull in a black ditch with a rat that played peep-bo through either eye-socket – let them exercise their responsibility to that class of public and we'd see who laughed the loudest. Do you know what I'm talking about?

MRS HIGGINBOTTOM. Talking about – no. But I'll tell you what I think –

UNDER-CONSTABLE. Not when we're on duty, Mabel: Mr Hopkins does the thinking here.

CONSTABLE. Mr Hopkins' cogitations at the moment are upon an improperly dressed subordinate. I am about to request you, Higginbottom, to perform a routine function and I want those legs concealed!

UNDER-CONSTABLE. Yes, Mr Hopkins. Come on, don't you hear him – is it threaded yet or isn't it? You can mend it while I'm wearing it. You make me proper ridiculous.

He puts on his torn trousers and MRS HIGGINBOTTOM *starts to sew them up.*

CONSTABLE (*to* LUKE). Flanders? It's a long way. And you've come here upon foot. With no apparent occupation nor yet means of support. Who are you, what's your business?

LUKE.

> I am a soldier of the King returned from the war
> And here in green England I will live for evermore.

CONSTABLE. Carry on then, give details. We've had enough rhyming clap-trap for one afternoon.

LUKE. I was Adjutant's Ancient in the Second Battalion of the Twenty-Third Regiment, otherwise known as the Royal Loyals or the Grin-and-bear-it Grenadiers. I am furthermore the only survivor of the disastrous expedition – to the Low Countries – against the French – last year – do you remember? But we didn't meet no French. We met fever, we met starvation, pouring rain and flooded country. A third of us was dead already and another third too poorly to put one foot before the other. And then the French did come. Horse, foot, guns. In the early stages of their onfall I got a blow from a partisan on the corner of my forehead – here: observe the scar. When I recovered my senses I found myself alone among a great field of dead men. The entire English army. And there were some French and all. . . . So I came home. All alone and being sought for. I got across the sea, even. I was fortunate – there were smugglers, who took no heed to either party in a war that didn't concern them, but were ready and willing to carry a man that had gold. Don't ask me where I got that gold. There are inevitable deeds have been performed in Flanders this last year that no decent man should inquire after. But I paid them all I had and they brought me; here I am. I am on my way to London to obtain my discharge from the Army in a regular fashion.

CONSTABLE. And no doubt to get a pension.

LUKE. I have hopes.

CONSTABLE. Ah. But have you papers? What's your proof of your identity?

LUKE. Proof? Papers? Look, my friend, I am a man of many

trials, I have had experiences, I have told you what they were, I thought I saw you listening! And yet you ask of me for papers. Of course I've not got papers!

CONSTABLE. Then you're a vagrant. It's not allowed. I'm afraid I have no alternative but to ask you, as a purely routine matter, just to answer a few questions, you understand, and to assist the police, and finally, to accompany me, and my subordinate here, with as little fuss as possible, into the lock-up.

(*During the pauses for punctuation in the above-speech, the* CONSTABLE *and* UNDER-CONSTABLE *have punched* LUKE *in the stomach with their truncheons, slapped him with the edge of their hands across the back of his neck, tripped him at the ankles, twisted his arms behind his back, and generally reduced him to a state of semi-consciousness. Taken by surprise and winded, he has made small resistance.*)

There we are, Higginbottom, fasten him in.

He and the UNDER-CONSTABLE *set about constructing a gaol round* WILLIAM *and* LUKE *until they are surrounded.* WILLIAM'S *handcuffs are removed. The ensuing dialogue continues during this business.*

WILLIAM. Hey, wait a minute, you can't treat him like that.

CONSTABLE. Can't we? We have.

MRS HIGGINBOTTOM. They have.

WILLIAM. I'm a witness. I saw it. You just knocked him down and stamped on him.

CONSTABLE. I'll stamp on you too.

MRS HIGGINBOTTOM. He'll stamp on you too.

WILLIAM. It's a gross abuse, it's brutality. I'm quite certain it's not allowed.

CONSTABLE. Vagrancy's not allowed. Performing filthy plays is not allowed neither.

MRS HIGGINBOTTOM. No, it's not, neither.

The gaol is now completed by the addition of a barred door.

CONSTABLE. So there you are, in.

MRS HIGGINBOTTOM. In.

CONSTABLE. And there you will stay until an opportunity arises to haul you both forth and present you to the magistrates. Did you take off his cuffs, Higginbottom?

UNDER-CONSTABLE. I did.

CONSTABLE. Come on then, where are they – we may want them for someone else? It's our red-letter day by the look of it today, we don't want to be held up in any further good work by the lack of essentials, what did you do with 'em, lad?

UNDER-CONSTABLE. I'm not entirely sure, I think I put them –

MRS HIGGINBOTTOM (*holding them up*). Here!

CONSTABLE. Right, we'll leave 'em to it.

(*He and the* HIGGINBOTTOMS *retire to the side of the stage.*)
Now you set down and keep your eyes upon 'em. Don't stand no nonsense, comply with no requests. We've not had many regular prisoners in before, so don't let your ignorance of correct procedure be took advantage of. In the meantime I shall make a tour of inspection of the parish and its boundaries: if there's any more misconduct, as it might be, infected by the bad examples we've already had, I shall know how to deal with it.

Exit CONSTABLE.

LUKE (*recovering his senses*). Oo – ouf – stamped upon . . . Kicked . . . Truncheoned in the gut . . . Oh: you're here as well, are you – bold St George for Merry England. Well, they say every blessed country gets the patron saint it deserves. I only hope your holiness is satisfied with the reception you're afforded.

WILLIAM. Really, you know, there is no need to taunt me. At least I was arrested trying to do a job of work, while all you were doing was –

LUKE. Begging – to be frank – vagrancy – quite true.

I gave all my filthy lucre
To the captain of the hooker
For a trip across the tide.
I couldn't ha' done worse
If I'd stayed on the far side.
At least in the midst of a war
A man whose clothes are tore
And whose legs are muddy
And his hands all bloody
Is greeted by the populace
With a degree of some respect.
They give you what you ask for, there,
So long as you ask for it direct
And when you've taken what you want to,
Off they scapa, double pronto.

I've got a cavern inside me – how's it going to get filled?
Do we get no rations, Mister, while we're stuck in your –

UNDER-CONSTABLE. No. I've no authority. Anything you've got to say can be said before the magistrates.

MRS HIGGINBOTTOM. Unless, I suppose –

UNDER-CONSTABLE (*as she prompts him in a whisper*). Unless, I suppose, you are prepared to make a statement. I believe that's important, and I fancy that betwixt us, we could get it written down.

MRS HIGGINBOTTOM. We could get it written down.

LUKE. Statement? Written down? Here we go then. Are you ready? Got your notebook? Got your pencil?

(*The* HIGGINBOTTOMS *search frantically to assemble these materials.*)

I, being of sound mind and both sober and responsible for my actions, am also – are you with me – am also downright hungry, and I'd be very much obliged if you'd –

UNDER-CONSTABLE. Oh no, that's not a statement.

LUKE. Yes it is.

MRS HIGGINBOTTOM. No it's not.

UNDER-CONSTABLE. No it's not. That's not a statement. That's Anything to Say, that, and it can be said before the magistrates, whom you will confront in – what is it?

MRS HIGGINBOTTOM. Due course.

UNDER-CONSTABLE. Don't you see? Mr Hopkins has a book, it's got rules in –

MRS HIGGINBOTTOM. Rules in. We're the Law.

UNDER-CONSTABLE. You've got to do like what we tell you. (*Enter* ESMERALDA *with a parcel.*)

This is private. Go away. Mr Hopkins says it's private.

MRS HIGGINBOTTOM. Yes he does, it's private.

ESMERALDA. Please –

UNDER-CONSTABLE. Oh no – it won't do – oh, look at her, love, she's crying –

MRS HIGGINBOTTOM. Oh dear, what a shame – poor girl, who can she be?

ESMERALDA. Please, your honour, my poor brother – I've followed him for miles and miles, I've been sent by my dear mother to bring him home to an honest life again, oh, William, my dearest William, how can you fall so low! Oh, William, leave this dreadful theatrical career and come home unto your dear ones, come home with me, William, today, for all has been forgiven!

MRS HIGGINBOTTOM. Oh my poor child, this is so sad and so true, he has fallen very low indeed.

UNDER-CONSTABLE. Is this lady your sister?

WILLIAM. My what?

UNDER-CONSTABLE. Is she your sister?

WILLIAM. Well, er, yes, if she says so.

UNDER-CONSTABLE. Then I hope you are ashamed to have brought her down to such a state.

WILLIAM. Oh yes, it's quite mortifying, I really am struck dumb.

ESMERALDA. Come home, then, come home with me – William, come home – don't just stay there but come!

WILLIAM. Esmeralda, do be practical – how on earth can I come home?

ESMERALDA. But I am sure they will let you go when I tell them that all has been forgiven. His poor mother has forgiven him everything, sir, everything, even the theft of the family pawntickets, which – poor boy – he didn't mean to take, only that he needed a little morsel of dry bread for his journey. Please let him come!

UNDER-CONSTABLE. I shall have to ask Mr Hopkins.

ESMERALDA. Do you think he will be lenient? But of course he will, if you will plead for us. Oh, Mrs –

UNDER-CONSTABLE. Higginbottom.

ESMERALDA. Oh, Mrs Higginbottom, you are a – you are a mother, are you not? This is a mother's cake. Baked by my poor mother and salted with her tears. Let him take it, while he's waiting for – for Mr –

MRS HIGGINBOTTOM. Hopkins –

ESMERALDA. His permission? Your permission. Just a cake. Made with eggs. Keep his strength up. You're a mother?

MRS HIGGINBOTTOM. Just a cake.

UNDER-CONSTABLE. Just a minute. Didn't I see you –

ESMERALDA. No. That was –

WILLIAM. My sister. With the actors.

UNDER-CONSTABLE. But this is your sister?

ESMERALDA. No. Not the same one. That was Chloe. I am Esmeralda. Chloe, dreadful girl, has not yet been forgiven. I am sorry to tell you that it was more than pawntickets in her case. Much more. Oh yes. *She* has been struck out.

WILLIAM. Struck out of what?

ESMERALDA. The family Bible, William, and so will you be too unless you do what I tell you and keep your mouth shut at once! There, can I give it him?

WILLIAM. Who made it?

ESMERALDA. Me.

WILLIAM. Ugh! Darling, ask me anything, but don't ask me to eat your cooking.

She passes the cake into the gaol and hurries out. WILLIAM *gives it scornfully to* LUKE. ESMERALDA *runs full tilt into the* CONSTABLE *who is returning.*

CONSTABLE. Ho ho, what have we here? Illicit visiting – contraband consignments – sneaking in and snooping round! Come into the light, young lady, explain yourself directly. Tears, tears, tears, she's half-hysterical. Higginbottom, what *have* you been permitting, the minute my back was turned?

UNDER-CONSTABLE. Compassionate reasons, Mr Hopkins, I can't really see there was any real objection –

MRS HIGGINBOTTOM. No real objection, poor soul, and all the pawntickets –

CONSTABLE. And what did she hand in to him, hey?

UNDER-CONSTABLE. Cake.

CONSTABLE. A what?

MRS HIGGINBOTTOM. Cake.

CONSTABLE. A what's that?

ESMERALDA. Cake!

CONSTABLE. Shut up, you'll blow me ears out. Cake, indeed . . . It's not allowed. At least it's not, without a proper payment. Half a crown or six fat kisses. Which?

ESMERALDA. I – I haven't any money . . . please, sir, please . . .

CONSTABLE. You haven't? . . .

(*He starts to kiss her.*)

Ooh, theatricals, how the blood boils over – a fair disgrace to the morals of the nation – ye-es . . .

Enter CROKE.

CROKE. Sir, unhand that lady! This is no office for an officer, restrain yourself for shame!

CONSTABLE. I thought I ordered you to remove yourself from this vicinity.

CROKE. Why, yes, you did. And so I was in process of so doing. But lo, a messenger, spurring his foundered horse along the highroad, rears to a halt and cries – 'Are you the actors?' 'Certainly we are.' 'Then here, 'says he. 'A letter, from the King!'

CONSTABLE. A letter from the King?

CROKE. The King.

UNDER-CONSTABLE. The King?

MRS HIGGINBOTTOM. The King?

CONSTABLE. For you?

CROKE. For me, Marcus Antonius Croke, tragedian – also comedian, and acrobat, and irregular entertainer. Read it – if you can.

He hands the CONSTABLE *a scroll of parchment.*

CONSTABLE. His Majesty's Privy Council . . . why, it's a Royal Pardon . . . all actors, players, buffoons, jesters, minstrels, tumblers and mountebanks . . . to be permitted, despite all offences committed against whomsoever . . . to be permitted, requested and required to go to London directly . . . in order, in order, to present plays before the King. . .! Have you just confected this—you and your confederates?

CROKE. Do I possess the Great Seal of the Realm?

CONSTABLE. H'm – and what am I supposed to do?

CROKE. Release him from his durance vile! William, my child, we are commanded, by His Majesty – our company entire – fame at last, success, high privilege – step forth, and come to London!

CONSTABLE. His Majesty, in my opinion, is most sadly deluded. But the Great Seal is the Great Seal and certainly outweighs such local applications of the Law as may be vested in my humble self. Higginbottom, let him out – in silence, if you please. I have a difficulty in finding words to fit this most deplorable contingency.

MRS HIGGINBOTTOM. Deplorable.
CONSTABLE. Be quiet.

The UNDER-CONSTABLE *opens the gaol and lets* WILLIAM *out.*

ESMERALDA (*embracing him*). Dear William –
CROKE. Come to my arms – not yours, you're not the Manager!

LUKE *has also walked out.*

UNDER-CONSTABLE. Where are you going – ?
LUKE. To stretch my legs. I thought maybe . . .

He returns as the CONSTABLE *appears about to charge at him. The cell is locked again.* CROKE *beckons* ESMERALDA *and* WILLIAM *impatiently.*

CROKE. William, we are off to act before the King! Buck up, girl, for heaven's sake. Come.

He stalks out, arm in arm with WILLIAM.

ESMERALDA (*to* LUKE).
  You look hungry.
  Eat the cake.
  Don't be angry
  If you break
  A tooth or two
  Upon the crust.
  A starving man
  Eats what he must –
  Who knows,
  It may be good for you?

She goes out.

LUKE (*calling after her*).
  This kindness I will not forget.
  Behind hard iron they hold me yet:

A hand can open what a hand can shut
And that stays true of every gate.
I will repay you soon or late.

CONSTABLE. Let us not, Mr Higginbottom, consider that our work has been rendered, by this injudicious interference from a higher authority, entirely null and void. We still have one prisoner in custody, and by the time I have organized my evidence against him, he is going to catch it hot. I intend to create for myself in this district a reputation as a scourge of evil-doers which will resound beyond our boundaries. I tell you in confidence that I have ambitions extending far in advance of rural misdemeanours. Have you ever considered the possibilities open to a talented man like me if once my zeal and initiative can be satisfactorily noised abroad? London, Mrs Higginbottom, is the goal of my aspirings – and not merely a job there pounding the pavements and keeping a check on the drunks and disorderlies – no. I want to be a regular thief-taker – undercover, incognito – a Detector is the word they use. You'll have heard of them, I dare well say –

They creep and creep in dark disguise
And track down crime by secret ways
With a great big hat pulled over their eyes –
All is concealed till the end of the story
And then, at the end – ha ha, the surprise:
For the rogue, the knotted rope –
For him that catches him, the glory!

What's the time?

UNDER-CONSTABLE. Quarter past.

MRS HIGGINBOTTOM. To.

UNDER-CONSTABLE. It's a quarter summat, anyway. Does that tally with yours?

CONSTABLE. It tallies with my stomach. My dinner will be smouldering. So you keep guard while I get off – I'll be back in fifty minutes.

Exit CONSTABLE.
LUKE *has been eating the cake. In it he has found a file.*

UNDER-CONSTABLE. His dinner will be smouldering. What about mine?

MRS HIGGINBOTTOM. Cold meat pie, so there's no bother.

UNDER-CONSTABLE. Go and get it then, I'll eat here.

MRS HIGGINBOTTOM. Get it yourself, can't you, and leave me on the watch. You know I always like to keep an interest in your work. Besides, you'll want a beer and I don't like going into the public if I can possibly avoid it – there's all them rakish fellers there what look at me conspicuous.

UNDER-CONSTABLE. I suppose it's all right – Mr Hopkins did say –

MRS HIGGINBOTTOM. Mr Hopkins won't be back till he's eat his roast and Yorkshire. Fifty minutes was his word – a slice of pie takes five. Get on.

Exit UNDER-CONSTABLE.
LUKE *grins at* MRS HIGGINBOTTOM *through the bars.*

LUKE. Cold enough for you, mum?

MRS HIGGINBOTTOM. You eat your cake.

LUKE. Draughty, though. I'm perished.

MRS HIGGINBOTTOM. On account of the bars. Mr Hopkins had them put in with gaps in between them, for to see what was going on inside, do you see? He said it's for security.

LUKE. Good of you to tell me so, mum, I appreciate a bit of information, when provided free of charge and outside of the routine minimum.

MRS HIGGINBOTTOM. Oh yes, there's no objection to a bit of a chat, I suppose.

LUKE. But it rattles, don't you see? It's not what I'm used to. I mean, I've had a hard life, as you'll appreciate, in the army, but this locality is peaceable, thanks to you and Mr Hopkins, and we don't need a noise going on all the night

from a rattling doorlatch – twice as loud as musket volleys –
I tell you no falsehood, mum.

MRS HIGGINBOTTOM. I don't know there's anything *I* can do
– you'd best wait until –

LUKE. Here though, I've got a notion. I thought – if you'd
assist me, being a good strong woman with a generous pair
of hands – I could just smooth the surface of this bolt where
it fastens, then it fits a little easier and it makes a sight less
clatter. If you took the other end of this file I've got here, you
could pull and I'll push and we'd do the job in half the time.

MRS HIGGINBOTTOM. Oh, I see now – you want it this way?
(*She helps him file the latch.*)
Quite a practical lad, aren't you? I don't suppose Higginbottom would have thought of a dodge like this. Nasty noisy
door, it's quite a shame to put you next it, I couldn't bear it
meself if I had to sleep there.

LUKE (*as the latch gives way*). Oh darn it, it's broke.

MRS HIGGINBOTTOM. Oh, now you've done it. Now you've
wrecked it. You'll be in trouble over this, you know. You'll
have to pay for this, you will, when Mr Hopkins gets back.

LUKE. Put a bit too much pressure on. I never thought it
wouldn't take an ordinary expenditure of muscular force –
isn't that what you're up against every day with these iron-
mongers – shoddy careless workmanship – here, you pop
inside, mum, and just see if you can't fix it from in there
while I have a look at the outside of these hinges . . .

*They change places. While she is fiddling with the latch he
creeps away.*

MRS HIGGINBOTTOM. Oh no, you've done it now. You've
gone and spoiled this lock completely. It's Government
property, you know, and there'll be forms to be filled in and I
don't know at all who's going to have to sort it out – oh
where on earth is Higginbottom, why don't he come and
help with it?

Enter HIGGINBOTTOM *with a pie, and a bottle of beer.*

UNDER-CONSTABLE. What's the matter, Mabel, I thought I heard you shouting . . . ? Good evening.

LUKE. Good evening, Constable, it's cold.

UNDER-CONSTABLE. Fair perishing, I'll take my oath.
(*He sees what has happened.*)
Hey wait a minute, come back here –

He runs after LUKE, *who finds no exit the way he is going and doubles back – only to run into the* CONSTABLE *coming in the other side. General confusion and dodging about the stage. In the course of this,* LUKE *seizes the pie and bottle from the* UNDER-CONSTABLE *and tackled by the* CONSTABLE, *fells him with a blow from the bottle and makes his escape.*

UNDER-CONSTABLE. Oh my lord, he's hit the Constable!

MRS HIGGINBOTTOM. Who has? Broken off short and the screw lost as well, it's going to need a blacksmith.

UNDER-CONSTABLE. A blacksmith – more like an undertaker – I think he's killed him, woman!

MRS HIGGINBOTTOM. Oh! It's Mr Hopkins! It's Mr Hopkins – he's been bashed!

CONSTABLE (*recovering*).
Felonious assault would be the correct description
For a blow of this nature, of deliberate infliction.
Indeed, I would go further –
See, I write it down as a case of attempted murder.
The murder of a badged and buttoned Constable
Is of all crimes of violence by far the most considerable.
The man who would commit it is a danger to the State.
The Law has rightly provided him an inexorable fate.
Nought shall prevent him being tracked down and found
Whether upon English ground
Or upon the soil of France or Spain.
I shall not turn again

Till I have caught him and brought him
To the foot of the gallows.
Wherever he may go, remorseless vengeance follows,
In disguise, close behind him,
Till with chains and ropes I bind him.
I shall not give over
Till he lies beneath the clover.

(*He takes off his badge and gives it to the* UNDER-CONSTABLE.)
Here, you take this: you'll want it. Clue Number One: he
grabbed your meat pie. It's a good thing your good lady
here makes her pastry so very flaky. There's bits of it dropped
all over the stage. Couldn't be easier if it was a regular paper-
chase. Here's a crumb and there's a crumb: and here's a
crumb and there's a crumb: and here's a crumb, and another
crumb, and another crumb, and another crumb here, and
another, and another here . . .

He goes out, sleuthing.

MRS HIGGINBOTTOM. Did he take the beer and all?
UNDER-CONSTABLE. He did.
MRS HIGGINBOTTOM. Eh dear . . . we might as well dis-
mantle. It's not much use keeping up a gaol if there's nobody
to put in it and the lock being broke and everything, did he
leave you his badge?
UNDER-CONSTABLE. He did. So I'm Chief Constable. I
suppose we'd best go home – we don't want to look for
trouble, do we?

*They go off, dismantling the gaol and taking the bars with them.
Enter* LUKE. *He is carrying the pie – half-eaten already.*

LUKE. Being a man of some initiative and considerable self-
respect, I find my situation particularly irksome. In Flanders,
you'd expect it. But this is old warm-hearted England that
sent me forth to fight and welcomes me now home again with
iron bars and truncheons and the sort of coarse contempt for

years of service that you'd scarcely look to find in – in the
deserts of Siberia. At least in such deserts, there are, as I have
been told, bands of wandering Tartars who would extend
the hospitality of their tents to the homeless hunted fugitive.
Hello, there's someone coming . . .

(*He turns his red coat inside out.*)

> No time now for foolish pride;
> Let the glory lurk inside.
> Here's a useful place to hide –
> Open eye and open ear –
> Oh oh, I've seen this lot before.
> Gipsies or beggars or a tribe of Tartar horse,
> I think if I went much further
> I might do a great deal worse.

He conceals himself as the ACTORS *enter, to rehearse (with
refreshments.).*

CROKE. The tragedy of *King Arthur*. Certainly it merits a re-
vival, does it not?

MRS CROKE. In the days when we played regularly before the
nobility and gentry, *King Arthur* was by far the most popular
piece in our repertoire. It is really so wonderful to have the
opportunity once more of putting on these fine old classics.
Antonius, do you think His Majesty would prefer –

CROKE. I am quite sure, my dearest love, that His Majesty
would prefer us all to be word-perfect. So let us run it
through, here in this convenient meadow, and waste no
more time. You can play the King, my boy.

WILLIAM. The lead, Mr Croke?

CROKE. It is the title-part, dear William, yes.

ESMERALDA. Sir Lancelot's part is longer and a good deal
more sympathetic.

CROKE. Of course it is, my dear – of course it is, dear William,
but really you can't complain if the manager decides for once
to stand upon his rights and eat a bit of the fat of the ham. I

mean, frankly there are two magnificent male parts in this play and any actor worth his salt should be only too happy to attempt either one of them. You *are* happy, aren't you? Have a sandwich. My dear, what have you here – can I believe my eyes – it is, it is –

MRS CROKE. A bottle of wine. I thought that some small celebration of our great good fortune might not be out of order. It is such a beautiful morning, with the birds and the daisies and the cows in the pasture – are there cows?

CLOWN. There have been.

MRS CROKE. Oh Charles, you might have mentioned it before – now you've quite spoiled the rehearsal – I wonder if we shouldn't move –

CROKE. Certainly not, we're very well as we are. Shall we start work? I'd like to run through that very lovely scene where Sir Lancelot first declares his forbidden love for Queen Guinevere. You remember it – my dear – in the garden, under the rose-trellis.

MRS CROKE. Indeed I do remember it – also do I remember the very first time you and I played that touching scene together, Antonius – it was at a special gala performance – my dears – in the courtyard of the Duke of Grosvenor's castle upon the occasion of the seventy-seventh birthday of the dear Duchess of Grosvenor. The Duke of course had his own private company of actors – alas long since disbanded by his unappreciative successors – and Antonius and I had been called in for this particular production, very specially, upon the recommendation of Lord and Lady de Brack – I remember oh so clearly how Lady de Brack said to her daughter – 'Clarissa, my darling, do you not agree with me that when one sees Mrs Croke as Guinevere one really knows at last what it is to be a woman?' Ah, those days are gone, and the water that has run beneath the bridges since has been by no means fresh and clear – but perhaps at long last we are coming once again into our own?

LUKE (*aside*). I wish they would come once again into the play.
At this rate they'll have nothing to put on before the King
but the litter of a picnic. Very agreeable picnic – I wouldn't
dispute that – ah, there's worse work in the world than being
an actor, it appears.

CROKE (*jumping up decisively*). Yes, well, now then, to work!
Scripts, Esmeralda darling, scripts, properties, we need the
rose-trellis, where is it? Set it up, my dear, no delays now –
we rehearse!

(ESMERALDA *hands out scripts and brings in the trellis, which
is rather shaky and she finds it difficult to erect it.*)

Guinevere, sitting down. Lancelot beside her, thus, the
palm of his hand upon the back of her hand, thus – I think
that's how we used to play it. We'll start from 'a double
passion'. Don't bother with the trellis, child, it's only
making difficulties, we'll carry on without. Ha ha, let me
see –

A double passion wars within my breast.
Now that my love for thee has been confessed
My duty to King Arthur must needs fly.
He is my Lord, for whom I once would die.
Alas, he is thy husband too. 'Tis plain
If I am not his enemy, he is mine.

MRS CROKE.

Nay, should he find us here, his angry blade
Must pierce thy heart and thou on turf be laid.
Sweet knight, there is such peril in thy devotion.
I sorely fear it will destroy this nation.

CROKE.

Yet am I not still loyal to the crown?
I swear it, by this rose that I pluck down!

No, no, it's altogether too difficult to do it without props.
I must have the rose – I have to smell it and kiss it, and put
it in your bosom and so forth – trellis, Esmeralda, trellis, if
if you please. The imagery of the rose is of prime importance

to this scene – William, are you watching? You may find yourself playing Lancelot one of these days; learn, me boy, learn – there's a tradition in this part, you know, as in all the great classic parts – we ignore it at our peril.

(ESMERALDA *has set up the trellis.*)

Good, good, try again –

I swear it, by this rose that I pluck down –!

(*In endeavouring to pluck the rose from the trellis, he finds it is too firmly fastened on. The whole trellis sways dangerously.*)

Oh, for heaven's sake – when was this last used? Who's been looking after the props? Esmeralda, really, this is frankly quite ridiculous! I cannot possibly continue with this scene until the whole thing's been overhauled. Not just now, dear, not just now – we'll carry on from somewhere else. We'll get on to the discovery. Mordred, the villain, brings in King Arthur to observe the guilty couple. William, are you ready? I'll give you your cue:

But hark, I hear a footstep on the sward.

No matter, I have my weapon, I am on guard.

William, I am on guard. But against whom, might I ask?

WILLIAM. It's not quite King Arthur yet. Mordred comes on first.

CROKE. Well, where is he? Where is Mordred?

ESMERALDA. You haven't cast him yet, Mr Croke.

CROKE. Oh. Charles. Leave those sandwiches alone for a moment, and pick up a script.

CLOWN. What, me, to play the villain?

MRS CROKE. Impossible. Do have some sense, Antonius. This isn't a comic villain, you know. I don't see how Charles can conceivably –

CROKE. Then who do you suggest, my love? We are but a small company.

ESMERALDA. I'll have a go. I've played breeches parts before. And he is meant to be a young man. Is that all right? Shall I enter? Mr Croke?

CROKE. Can you fight? There is a battle in the last act. Otherwise I don't –

MRS CROKE. Let her try it, at any rate. You'd better take your skirt off.

(ESMERALDA *takes off her skirt – she has tights on under it.*)
She'll have to double with the lady-in-waiting in Act Two – I must have the lady-in-waiting or my entire hysterical scene will go for nothing. Remember I have to slap her, it's my best moment in the whole play. So carry on, my dear, roll your eyes and don't forget to swagger. You'll be wearing a sword-belt, of course.

CROKE. Just one moment. If Esmeralda is going to play the villain, and really, you know, there is no reason why she shouldn't because apart from the battle it's not a very large part – who is going to be Merlin?

MRS CROKE. Can we not cut Merlin, my love?

CROKE. I don't think so – he's most important – he has to warn Lancelot about the – no no, we can't cut him. It would be better to cut the lady-in-waiting if we have to . . . I have it. I can double Merlin with Lancelot, play it myself. A white beard, sky-blue mantle, throw it over my armour – the character is attractive – sophisticated, whimsical, rather terrifying when he prophesies. I've never played him. It's a challenge.

ESMERALDA. They have a conversation.

CROKE. Who has a conversation?

ESMERALDA. Merlin and Lancelot. They have a conversation.

MRS CROKE. So you can't play them both.

CROKE. Esmeralda, this is a classical poetical tragedy. The Dramatis Personae do not have 'conversations'. Their dialogue is couched in a splendour of language, which –

MRS CROKE. Which leaves us with Charles, who is the only member of the company not yet provided with a part.

WILLIAM. It is possible, of course, we have chosen the wrong play.

MRS CROKE. I had set my heart on playing Guinevere before the King and all his Court.

CLOWN. Tell you what, I'll send him up a bit. You know, make him a kind of absent-minded professor type – his magic spells always going wrong and losing his spectacles, that kind of thing. Supposing he should have got muddled with one of his enchantments and every time he comes in he has to roll in upside down – like this – you see, he's lost his centre of gravity – hilarious really – besides, we need a bit of comic relief if we're on in front of royalty – they can't stand the heavy stuff, get far too much of that in their ordinary life. Look, I'll do it again, just to show you, what do you think of it – ?

CROKE. No. This is classical poetical tragedy. We cannot possibly –

MRS CROKE. Indeed we cannot. So what is the solution ?

LUKE *comes forward.*

LUKE. Me. I'm not precisely whimsical, and certainly not sophisticated. But the terrific prophecy bit ought not to be too difficult. My voice is well trained, having had experience of half the parade grounds in England, let alone three-quarters of the battle-fields of Europe, and my physique is well adapted to any running, jumping, stamping or strutting that may be in request. I don't expect you to take me straight away without an opportunity to shew what I can do: but give me a script and half a moment to study it and I'll let you have an earful . . . By the way, if there's any sword-fighting in the part, you've got the very man. Luke is the name – or the first part of it anyway – I'd better not tell you the rest of it: for personal reasons, which I dare say *you* (*To* ESMERALDA.) can guess at, I prefer to remain anonymous. Right then, what about it ?

CROKE. We are not conducting auditions, my dear sir. This

company is already complete. Thank you very much – good morning.

LUKE. I am sorry I intruded.

He retires but does not actually go away.

CROKE. Admittedly an extra man would be very useful but I have no intention of lowering our standards by taking on non-professionals. Particularly in view of this most important engagement. Charles: you will play Merlin and you will play it with dignity. Give him a script. First entrance in the garden once again. Lancelot and the King have quarrelled, Lancelot has fled, Queen Guinevere sits weeping – sit weeping, my dear – that's right – and Arthur is talking with Sir Mordred about – ah –

ESMERALDA.

> The need to kill your most unfaithful wife,
> Whose crime has brought upon this land cruel strife.
> The blood of one will save the blood of all.
> Condemn her: let the sword of justice fall!

CROKE. Not at all bad, my dear. But roll your eyes a bit more. You're not entirely sincere, you know – you *want* a civil war – you are *dissembling* with the King. Carry on, William.

WILLIAM.

> I have loved this wicked woman since I was but a boy.
> If I kill her I kill my pride and joy.
> Why is not Merlin here? He would advise
> Some deed to do both merciful and wise.

CROKE. Now then, Charles, let's see what you *can* do.

CLOWN. Alas! The great Round Table is no more.

CROKE. You sound like a broken-down pensioner at the gate of the alms-houses. Never mind pretending to be a doddery old man. You're supposed to be a genius, an intellectual – a sage! I know it is not easy for you, Charles, but it ought to be not entirely impossible. Try it again.

CLOWN.

> Alas! The great Round Table is no more.
> Those knights so bold who numbered fifty score
> Scattered, confused, their loyalties divided,
> Some stand on one side, some on the other, some
> stand astride it –

CROKE. What!

CLOWN. One party thus, another party thus, and another in
middle,

> And now I've split me breeches and I've fallen in a
> puddle!

MRS CROKE. I don't know how that got into the script, but it is
out from this moment!

CLOWN. I'm sorry, Mr Croke – but –

CROKE. Carry on!

CLOWN.

> My magic arts may yet put all things right.
> Observe these roses blooming, red and white –
> See, I will –

I can't do it without the rose-trellis, Mr Croke.
Esmeralda, be a darling – just hold it up for me –

> See I will strike them with my enchanted wand,
> And as their petals fall upon the grateful ground
> So shall forgetfulness flood into your sad mind.
> But one is plucked already. That is bad.
> By whom?

No it isn't – it's still there. Lancelot should have plucked it. I
have to find it on the grass, don't I? Here, this one will do –
Half a mo, Mrs Croke, I won't inconvenience you more than
I have to –

*Tugging at a rose he brings down the whole trellis again, this
time on top of* MRS CROKE.

CROKE (*giving way to despair*). And this. And this, ladies and
gentlemen, is the show we propose to put on – by Royal

Command – in London! I have never felt so disgraced in all
my life by so incompetent a collection of pier-end pierrots! I
think I shall disband the company. I shall do a one-man act
instead. I shall recite Homer's *Odyssey*, from end to end,
with no assistance, in the original Greek! At least I shall
know then whom to blame if things go wrong.

LUKE (*coming forward again*). Who's that then – yourself?

CROKE. No sir. Homer! . . . I would be very glad to know
what you think you are laughing at?

LUKE. Carpentry. Now, what you need is a good, stout pair of
battens, say four-by-two by two feet each, fixed here and
properly strutted. Hammer? Nails? Haven't you got any?
(ESMERALDA *goes and looks for them vaguely.*)
Don't you know? Give 'em to me then – let me handle it.
Practically nothing at all that I can't handle in the way of
tangible work and swift action in emergency. God knows,
I've had experience. All right, so it's turned me sour. My
manners as you might put it are a little bit abrupt. (*To*
ESMERALDA.)
But I think that you think that that might not perhaps be
altogether to my discredit. Am I right then? What do you say?

ESMERALDA (*sings*).
     'I stand alone against the world
     On two extended feet:
     I need no help from anyone
     To save me from defeat,
     Except a hammer, and a nail,
     And timber all complete:
     Oh please dear, could you find for me
     A piece of cake to eat –
     Oh please dear, could you find for me –'

LUKE. Cake? Oh no – I'm eating pie. *And* I went down upon
no knees to obtain it, I can tell you.

ESMERALDA. It's a question of ingredients. Sometimes one
can find in cake what you'd never discover outside of it.

LUKE. Oh yes, that's very true – by chance, one might so find. Now according to *my* philosophy, what one picks up by chance is there to be made use of: but it doesn't necessarily commit a man to a dependence upon anyone. Hold it firm for just a minute, that's right, and I'll jam the nail in this way – no point in elaborating the workmanship more than we have to . . .

WILLIAM. You seem to be elaborating it a fair amount already. We *were* in the middle of a rehearsal. How much longer do you think it's going to take?

LUKE. Now look here: your holiness: do you want this done or don't you? You've got yourselves landed with a pergola that won't stand up: as it so happens there's a man here that can mend it. Now which of the two are you going to stand fast by? It's all equal to me: I can take me pie and be off: you've only to say the word –

CROKE. There's no need to be offensive . . . I'm sure we all appreciate . . . I'd be very much obliged if . . . What do you think, my dear?

MRS CROKE. Perhaps if we were to continue the rehearsal at a little distance – over there – then we could safely leave this good man –

LUKE. Luke is the name, madam. As I told you. Recollect it?

MRS CROKE. Just so. As I was saying, we could safely leave Mr Luke to continue his good work, which I am sure we are very grateful for. Esmeralda, perhaps you would stay to give him a hand and fetch him anything he needs. We don't require you at the moment, my dear – we do, however, require *you*, Charles. And I will thank you to forget your usual vulgarity and pay proper attention to the text, if you please.

CLOWN. You can't teach an old dog new tricks, Mrs Croke –

MRS CROKE. Yes we can, and we mean to. Antonius, come.

Exeunt the CROKES, WILLIAM *and the* CLOWN.

ESMERALDA. I don't think they liked that.

LUKE. Liked what?

ESMERALDA. Well, the way you said it. You're too sharp with them. Good God, they're going to London to act before the King! They expect a deal more obsequiousness from an unemployed handyman.

LUKE. A handyman? On the tramp.

ESMERALDA. On the scrounge.

LUKE. Just like them, so where's the difference? Besides, I'm not, am I? I'm doing a job.

ESMERALDA. You don't expect to get paid?

LUKE. Why not? It's measurable. Time spent and skill laid out. They do pay *you*, I suppose?

ESMERALDA. Now and then.

LUKE. But you stay with them?

ESMERALDA. I've no choice. I was born into the business. And I don't know any other.

LUKE. None at all?

ESMERALDA. None at all. Well . . . none I care to follow. What about you?

LUKE. Ah, but I'm a soldier. That's exceedingly flexible. Soldier in a uniform once: soldier of fortune now. Which means I can be an actor as easily as anybody. So I am.

ESMERALDA. No you aren't.

LUKE. Stage-carpenter. It's the first step. I'm stuck in here and I'm staying. Have you any objections?

ESMERALDA. No. But I'm surprised. Did you desert from the army?

LUKE. It deserted from me. That'll do. No more questions. Now lend a hand with the work, can't you?

ESMERALDA. You don't give much away.

LUKE. I don't. I've learnt better. Just yesterday, my little love, I was taught a thorough lesson. I can still feel the marks of it – two inches below my belt!

ESMERALDA. Are you married, by any chance?

LUKE. I said: no more questions.

ESMERALDA. I did give you that cake.

LUKE. Ah yes. To let me free. Surely not to grip me tighter . . .
Yes, I am married. Twice. One of them's in Ireland: one
in Flanders. The one in Flanders was a stratagem. Being on
the run, you see, and short of cash. In both cases they had no
business believing a word they heard me say. Because when
all is said and done, a scrounging beggarman is not reliable.
And that means *you're* not. So I don't rely. But, being dressed
against my will in a dirty stinking cow-skin, I find it best to
walk upon four legs and not be too conspicuous. So I am taking
the risk and I'm joining your company. That is – supposing
old Sir Lancelot there – what's his real name?

ESMERALDA. Croke.

LUKE. Yes. Supposing croaking Lancelot should confirm me in
my new job – obsequious and degrading though it very well
may be – I intend to stay with it, until – until what? You're
on your road to London, right? To áct before the King,
right? Under precisely what circumstances – I mean, Royal
Pardons, and all that – surely it's not usual?

ESMERALDA. The son of the King of England is going to be
married to the daughter of the King of France, to celebrate
the end of the war.

LUKE. Ho, they call it a war, do they?

ESMERALDA. And what do you call it?

LUKE. A muck-up. I was part of it. Never mind, carry on.

ESMERALDA. And the wedding is going to be held in Paris.
And the King of France has offered a prize of one hundred
golden guineas to the best company of actors, either English
or French, to perform a play before him as a part of the
festivities. So our King, having, as you might imagine, no
proper actors of his own, has ordered all the companies in
England to come straightaway to London, and the ones that
do best in London will be sent across to France. It won't be
us, of course.

LUKE. Not unless you smarten your visual effects up, it won't.

You'll have gathered, I daresay, I have a pretty strong contempt for the standards of your profession.

ESMERALDA. Not a very flattering opinion. It's an honest one. You take my advice and keep quiet about it here; if you keep quiet we will. Even the Crokes will. They don't like the the police any more than you. I suppose that is what you're after?

LUKE. Keeping quiet?

ESMERALDA. Oh, about cake and all sorts of other things.

LUKE. Yes, you could put it that way.

You see, your Royal Pardon doesn't cover what I've done.

I am as you know a man on the run:

I must hide from my pursuers in whatever way I can.

I must construct for my own self my own dark secret place

Which might be on the stage with a mask upon my face,

Or it might be with the hammer and nails behind the scene.

But either way I cannot, I dare not, take part

In a gaudy public celebration of the beauties of art.

The best I can do is contribute in private

To the success of your troupe. If ever you arrive at

The King's Court in Paris, no doubt I could advance

And appear before the world as the equal of you all.

I cannot imagine they'll be seeking me in France:

But my danger is yet urgent. With your little file

I cracked the bar and broke the gaol:

I hit the Constable on the head:

If they catch me I'm as good as dead!

ESMERALDA. Go on, it's not true. It's like something out of one of our plays.

LUKE. Ah, that's just the way I tell it – I'm getting caught up with the atmosphere. General degeneration, you see, blurs the realities of life.

I hit the Constable on the head:

If they catch me I'm as good as dead!

Oh oh, look who's here!

ESMERALDA. Hide yourself – quick – behind the bushes or – somewhere –

LUKE. No no, this'll do . . .

He bends over a box of properties with his back turned as the CONSTABLE *enters, backwards, tracing bits of pastry.*

CONSTABLE. Here's a crumb, and there's a crumb and another crumb and another and a crumb here. (*He bumps his bottom into* LUKE'S *bottom. They both turn round.* LUKE *has put on the* CLOWN'S *mask.*) Hello hello hello – what's all this?

LUKE (*mimicking the* CLOWN). Hello hello hello – we don't require any milk this morning, thank you very much!

CONSTABLE. And what do you think you mean by milk?

LUKE. Ow I've split me – no no, no no, no no no, perfectly all right, Officer, not a stitch out of place! I thought for one terrible moment – oh, I still do – oh dear – let me see – (*He rolls over trying to see the seat of his pants.*)

Heel and toe go over head

To test the work of needle and thread.

In any case, we're out of your district now, you can't arrest us here. So take yourself off, my good man, double-quick time, poppity-pop!

CONSTABLE. That is perfectly correct as far as your trousers are in question. And talking of trousers – (*He is looking at Esmeralda's tights.*) Are you aware that it is not allowed to impersonate the opposite sex in public? If *I* can't arrest you, there'll be others that can. On a point of attempted murder, however, my jurisdiction is infinite. Where is the man with the meat pie? I've been a-following of his crumbs. All night.

LUKE. Crumbs. Was that the soldier?

CONSTABLE. So he described himself.

LUKE. Oh yes. Well, he ate his pie.

CONSTABLE. Here?

ESMERALDA. Here.

CONSTABLE. Here. Yes. That seems borne out by the circumstantial evidence.

LUKE (*surreptitiously wiping crumbs off his clothes*). And then he moved on.

CONSTABLE. Whither?

ESMERALDA. Thither.

CONSTABLE. To drown himself, no doubt? That road leads nowhere but the edge of the –

LUKE (*covering up by pointing in a different direction*). Thither.

CONSTABLE. I didn't say thither. I was about to say river.

LUKE and ESMERALDA (*together*). Ah yes, the river. Yes, to drown himself, no doubt.

CONSTABLE. He appeared to have something on his mind?

LUKE. On his mind? Oh Officer, he was –

ESMERALDA. Distracted with distress.

CONSTABLE. Remorse, of course, he would be. The bed of the river must forthwith be dragged. I shall go and find a boatman and we shall see what we shall see.

Exit CONSTABLE.
As soon as he goes the ACTORS *re-enter*.

CLOWN. Hey, you, take my face off.

CROKE. Never mind your face. Is the document safe?

LUKE *gives the mask to the* CLOWN *who puts it away, offended*.

ESMERALDA. The document, Mr Croke?

CROKE. The Royal Pardon, nitwit! You know who that man is who has just gone away. Why, he would like nothing better than to purloin that piece of parchment and then he would be able to arrest us once again. Without the Pardon we are nothing –

(ESMERALDA *finds it in the basket and gives it to him*.)

But with it in our safe possession, we are –

ALL. The King of England's Players!

They strike attitudes.

CROKE. Is the scenery ready, Mr Luke?

LUKE. If it is, sir, can I count myself engaged?

CROKE. As what?

LUKE. Stage carpenter, stage manager, property manager, scenic artist, wardrobe superintendent – whatever you like! Name it, sir, I'll do it!

CROKE. Then do it, Mr Luke – for we are to act before the King: we must present ourselves without a blemish.

Musical interlude, during which the scenery is set up – largely by LUKE *– and the* ACTORS *all put on their costumes and masks for the* 'King Arthur' *play. At the end of the music, they advance and bow, acknowledging applause. The* KING *and the* PRINCE *have entered behind the audience and they stand and bow graciously to the* ACTORS, *clapping with discretion.* LUKE *quietly withdraws. The* ACTORS *remove their masks.*

CROKE (*with emotion*). Your Majesty, Your Royal Highness, we are Your Majesty's most honoured and most faithful servitors, and for this opportunity which we have had tonight to act before Your Majesty in Your Majesty's own palace, we offer to Your Majesty our most unfeigned and humble gratitude.

The LORD CHAMBERLAIN *bustles through the audience and addresses the house.*

LORD CHAMBERLAIN. Ladies and gentlemen, the King has now seen examples of the work of all the English actors whom he has called into his presence. He is about to announce which of these many companies have pleased him the most, and which shall be the one to travel to France for the wedding of His Royal Highness. Are you all properly dressed to receive the King's decision? Are all your company present?

CROKE. All. Save of course the Stage Manager.

MRS CROKE. Surely, my love, we need not bother about him –
he is not –

LORD CHAMBERLAIN. Oh yes, indeed, madam, the King
desires to see everyone.

ESMERALDA. But he can't see the Stage Manager – *he* has to
stay behind scenes – he mustn't –

CROKE. Esmeralda, be silent. You are in the Royal Presence.
Of course the Stage Manager comes forward to be presented
to the King. He is part of our company, he must take his
proper place. It is insulting to His Majesty to put on such
false modesty. Mr Luke, forward!

While this has been going on, the KING *and the* PRINCE *have
come on to the stage. They talk in whispers to the* LORD
CHAMBERLAIN *with their backs turned to the* ACTORS.
The CONSTABLE *appears – dressed as a beefeater – in an
unexpected corner and speaks to the audience.*

CONSTABLE. I have been patrolling thus disguised through
the back corridors of the Palace. There was nobody at all at
the bottom of that river. Clearly the man I want has travelled
with these actors. Did not his very crumbs stop short beside
their resting place?

 I am now a true Detector:
 Oh, what glory I shall win
 If I track down my murderer
 In the presence of the King!

(LUKE *comes sheepishly forward in obedience to* CROKE, *sees the*
CONSTABLE *and abruptly retires.*)

 Goodness gracious, was that him –?
 I didn't have time to see.
 Never mind, I'm on the watch –
 It takes a clever lad to diddle *me*!
 Somewhere behind
 They have got him confined.

On my tiptoes prowl around,
Lurk with lug-hole to the ground,
His doom already is bespoken
His dirty neck already broken!

Exit CONSTABLE.
As soon as he goes out LUKE *re-enters with a false nose on.*

CROKE. Mr Luke, what on earth have you got there! Take it off at once!

LUKE. No no, if you'll excuse me, I have a very nasty boil upon my nose. His Majesty surely would not want to be confronted –

LORD CHAMBERLAIN. Ssh ssh – it's too late now. Stand very still and quiet and pray heaven the King won't notice.

KING (*to the* ACTORS). We have seen a great many plays in a great many days. We didn't like any of them at all, Mr – er –

CROKE. Croke, Your Majesty. Marcus Antonius Croke.

KING. Yes. None of them were funny and there were very few beautiful actresses – which is the only sort of thing I enjoy in the theatre. And the scenery in general was exceedingly shoddy. In fact yours was the only company whose scenery didn't quiver in the wind, let alone fall down, which happened to that deplorable lot we saw yesterday. Didn't it? Didn't it? Ridiculous. I don't know much about plays, but I do know a decent piece of construction when I see it. Pretty sound, this, really – what d'you think, me boy, hey? Who is your Stage Manager – he deserves congratulation?

CROKE. Stage Manager, Your Majesty . . . Here is the Stage Manager – he has a – has a boil upon his –

KING. Gad, you know – how droll! Some comedy at last! So you are an actor too, are you, are you, hey! But you did not perform? How's that – how is it?

LUKE. No, Your Majesty – not exactly perform – I – er I was to have –

ESMERALDA. He was to have spoken an epilogue, or speech

at the end, Your Majesty, but we didn't have time for it.

KING. No time? But your scenery proves you to be a real old-fashioned craftsman, we must certainly hear an epilogue from such an excellent and conscientious fellow – I think you have here a valuable member of your troupe, Mr Croke, am I right? First-class professional standards and no mistake about it. Carry on then, carry on.

CLOWN. He's not, of course, Your Majesty, the regular comic. Oh no, oh no, oh no. I should say not indeed. But let's have some equality, let's have some fair treatment. If you want some hilarity –

CROKE. If you want some hilarity, yes indeed, Your Majesty, we have here the very man. He does his little dance very deftly. Charles, do your little dance. Very deftly indeed, sir . . .

The CLOWN *dances with abandon: but he receives nothing but a cold glare from the* KING *and relapses into an embarrassed silence.*

PRINCE. Well. We are waiting. We are waiting for the epilogue.

KING. Do you not intend to deliver it at all?

LUKE. Er – very well, Your Majesty – yes.

CROKE. Oh good lord, this is the end. Our fortunes are all ruined.

MRS CROKE. How could you, Esmeralda!

LUKE. It's in the nature of a – do you see – of a tribute to the gallant soldiers who fought so well for Your Majesty in the recent wars in Flanders, now so happily concluded.

PRINCE. Very appropriate.

KING. Carry on.

LUKE.

> Starving though we were and tired and ill
> We never did forget our soldier's skill:
> We kept our boots clean and our bayonets bright,
> We waved our banners and we marched upright,
> We dared the French to meet us and to fight.

And when we met we fought till none could stand.
Our bodies now lie in a foreign land,
Defeated, they have said. But we know better:
We obeyed our general's orders to the letter.
If blame there is to be – indeed we did not win –
Blame not your loyal soldiers, gracious King,
But blame those ministers, who sitting warm at home
Sent us across the seas, unfed, unclothed, alone,
To do our duty the best way that we could.
We did it, sir, by pouring out our blood.
There is no more to say.

LORD CHAMBERLAIN. Indeed there is no more to say. I have
never in all my life heard such insolence before His Majesty.
Do you desire me, my lord, to throw him into prison?

KING. Prison? What do you think, me boy? Shall we throw
him into prison? Or shall we send him to Paris?

PRINCE. I think we would do better if we invited him to
become a member of the Government, father. At least he
appears to have some common sense and humanity, which is
more than your ministers generally can boast.

KING. We won't go into that now. But Gad it was a good
speech, most courageously delivered. Shall you speak so
plain at the Court of the King of France? Shall you, shall
you, hey? I do hope so. We must remind them, must we not,
that though we may be forced to seek for peace, we rule over
a people who are bold, free, independent, and downright
devilish awkward. Let those fellows over there forget that at
their peril. What? At their peril! Go to Paris, Mr Croke,
with your magnificent company, you will do credit to us all!
Very well, you may disperse.

(*The* KING *with the* PRINCE *and the* LORD CHAMBERLAIN
remove themselves a little way from the ACTORS, *who all
gather round* LUKE *and shake him by the hand.*)

Lord Chamberlain, how will the actors travel? In the same
ship as the Prince?

LORD CHAMBERLAIN. Their scenery and baggage will travel in the same ship as the Prince. There won't be room for the actors themselves. They will have to be provided with a vessel of their own.

The CONSTABLE *creeps in.*

KING. Well, see that it's a good one. The prestige of these fine artists is the prestige of the whole of England. Remember that.

CONSTABLE. Psst psst – Your Majesty – one moment – if you please.

LORD CHAMBERLAIN. Ssh ssh – go away – go away –

KING. And of course they will need passports. How many of them are there – six?

LORD CHAMBERLAIN. So it appears, my lord –

KING. Then issue six passports –

LORD CHAMBERLAIN (*handing the documents out of his satchel to the* ACTORS). There you are, six passports.

KING. And – er – enough money, of course, to cover the costs of the journey.

LORD CHAMBERLAIN (*handing them money*). Three and fourpence each, for travelling expenses.

CLOWN. Only three and fourpence and all the way to France? Quite fantastic. Are you sure that those are your instructions, my good man? Oh make it six and eightpence, there's a darling – do.

LORD CHAMBERLAIN. I take my orders from His Majesty and from nobody else. There, sir, are your expenses.

CLOWN. Ho, we'll see about that.

(*As the* KING *takes the* PRINCE *aside for a private word, the* CLOWN *sneaks up behind him, takes off the crown and puts it on his own head. He then addresses the* LORD CHAMBERLAIN [KING'S *voice*].*)

Lord Chamberlain, three and fourpence is most damnably stingy. Give them six-and-eight!

General sensation. The KING *turns to see himself confronted by what is apparently another monarch, and is completely at a loss for a moment.*

KING. What's that? Who are you? Good God, you've got my . . .

CLOWN. I'm sorry, I didn't really . . . A bit de-tropp really . . . It was just a . . .

KING. Off, sir.

CLOWN. Just a little . . .

PRINCE. Take it off, sir.

CLOWN. Gag . . .

LORD CHAMBERLAIN. Take it off at once!

KING. Mr Croke, is this usual?

CROKE. Your Majesty . . . he is instantly discharged from my employment. Charles, you are discharged.

MRS CROKE. Do you hear, Charles, you are discharged!

CLOWN. But you can't sack me. Who's going to play Merlin?

CROKE. *I* shall play Merlin.

KING. Give your passport back at once to the Lord Chamberlain and take yourself off. Or I'll clap you in irons.

The CLOWN *returns his passport and then kneels, pathetic, before the* KING *to ask for pardon. Suddenly he straightens up again.*

CLOWN. I've split me breeches!

He cartwheels off the stage.

KING. Good heavens, such behaviour! And now, if you will permit me, I desire to speak to my son.
(*The* ACTORS *bow, and disperse.*
The KING'S *eye falls on the* CONSTABLE.)
Who is this person? Lord Chamberlain, will you please ask him to wait.
(*The* LORD CHAMBERLAIN *moves the* CONSTABLE *away,*

but finds himself held by the buttonhole and forced to listen to an elaborate whisper. The KING *addresses the* PRINCE.)

Now, the Princess of France is a very beautiful woman. You are not to fall in love with her. You are only getting married, do you understand, in order to provide a year or two of peace between the two countries. When my army has had time to pull itself together after its unfortunate defeat, we shall once again go to war.

PRINCE. With the French?

KING. Of course with the French. Who else then, who else, hey? And this time, we shall win. When we go to war, you and your new wife obviously will not be able to live together: so you see, don't fall in love.

PRINCE. I shall take care to do whatever you say, father.

KING. Splendid, splendid! Of course you will. So: off you go. You have my blessing. Your retinue awaits. And don't let the King of France go taking advantage of you. Sound the trumpets, beat the drums, the Prince departs for Paris!

Exit the PRINCE, *to the sound of music.*
The KING *turns to the* CONSTABLE.

Now sir, what do you want?

LORD CHAMBERLAIN. It might be very important, my lord. This gentleman is a police officer, a thief-taker, he is at present in disguise. He says he is on the track of a murder.

KING. Gad, you don't tell me! What, in the Palace, in the Palace – where?

CONSTABLE. He is somewhere among those actors. I followed him across country and I am positive that he travelled here with them. Er – that is to say – milord.

KING. Which one of them is he?

CONSTABLE. Ah, there's the problem. You see, they *will* disguise their faces. It makes it very difficult. But the original Royal Pardon that got them out of trouble listed five persons and no more. Now your Lord Chamberlain here has just

given away six passports and no less. So, making an allowance
for that clown-chap that didn't give satisfaction and, very
rightly, had to go – we discover, by deduction, that there is
still an Extra Man.

KING. Oh, most acute of you. But it can't be helped, can it?
They are extremely good actors and they're all going to
France. I can't possibly hold them back. Who else am I
going to send? All the other theatrical companies were
absolutely terrible. Scenery tottering all over the shop.
England would be disgraced if such hobbledehoys appeared
in Paris. Croke's men have had their passports, and that's
enough of that. They have received our Royal Approval.
Have they not, Lord Chamberlain?

LORD CHAMBERLAIN. If you say so, sire. But who did he
kill?

CONSTABLE. Me, milord. That is –

KING. You? Come come, sir – you're no spectre. Here is my
fist – does it go through you? No.

CONSTABLE. Attempted was the word I was endeavouring to
articulate.

KING. Oho, so that is different. Indeed, it's very different.
Altogether, hey?

LORD CHAMBERLAIN. Altogether, yes. Murdering is one
thing, but attempted murder of an Officer –

KING. Good God, we can't have that! What are you waiting
for? Get after him, man. They've all gone to the harbour.
You must catch 'em before they sail. If they're on board ship
already, you'll have to hire a boat and follow them. Lord
Chamberlain, give him a passport: and give him fifty guineas,
for his travelling expenses.

(*The* LORD CHAMBERLAIN *does so. Prompted by a whisper
from the* CONSTABLE, *he makes a special note in the passport.*)
And another fifty guineas, if he finally gets his man!

    Our stern protective justice shall extend
    Into the very realm of France and thence

Haul back by force the villain who would dare
Lift hand against an Officer of mine!
Go forward, sir, be bold, you need not fear –
Your King defends the defenders of his power.

(*The* CONSTABLE *is hurrying out when the* KING *calls him
back.*)

But wait a moment, just come back – you must not arrest
him until the wedding is over, you know – we can't postpone
the wedding – international politics – very delicate – very
fragile, so you just watch it, do you hear? Find out who he is,
wait till the festivities are finished, and strike home at that
moment with all the Majesty of the Law. Very good – carry
on . . . no, look here, come back here – don't let anybody
in France know what you are there for. Bad for prestige . . .
isn't it, isn't it, what? . . . Well: what are you waiting
for . . ?

Exeunt.

Act Two

The ACTORS *are rowing across the sea to France in a boat.* LUKE
is not with them. ESMERALDA *stands in the stern at the tiller and
acts as shantyman.*

ESMERALDA (*sings; the others join in on the chorus-lines*).
     'For travelling expenses three and fourpence per head
      (Rowing over the sea to France)
     They'd pay more to the gravediggers when we are
      dead
      (If it blows up a gale we haven't a chance).
     The King's great Lord Chamberlain found us a boat
      (Rowing over the sea to France)
     But he couldn't be bothered to see if it would float
      (If it blows up a gale we haven't a chance).'

CROKE. We must be about in the middle by now. Can you see
the lighthouse at Calais ?

ESMERALDA. Not a sign of it, Mr Croke.

WILLIAM. I can't see the Dover lighthouse any longer, that's
something anyway.

ESMERALDA. We must be in the middle by now.

MRS CROKE. Very comforting to hear that, I'm sure, it's the
deepest part just here.

CROKE. Come on, sing up, can't you. We've got to keep going.

MRS CROKE. Oh dear, I feel so sick.

ESMERALDA (*sings*).
     'Right down underneath us the horrible monsters
      (Rowing over the sea to France)
     Are waiting for the water to crash in amongst us
      (If it blows up a gale we haven't a chance).'

WILLIAM. It's begun to crash in already – hasn't anyone got

a tin can or something – we shall have to bail the boat out.

CROKE. Use your hat, you blockhead, and save your breath for
your work.

MRS CROKE. Oh Antonius, do stop shouting so – my poor
head will split in three! Oh dear, I feel so sick.

WILLIAM. Use your hat, you blockhead, and save your breath
for the work.

MRS CROKE. What did you say, William? I will not permit
impertinence!

CROKE. Just you mind your manners when you are addressing
Mrs Croke! If you want to keep your job with this company,
my man –

ESMERALDA. Oh row, everybody, row – for heaven's sake, row
– do you want us all to be drowned?
(*Sings*).

'Indeed I am sure we do not want to drown
(Rowing over the sea to France) –'

I can't think of anything to rhyme with drown. Just carry on
singing the chorus until we get there . . .

They do so.

WILLIAM. Oh where the devil is Luke? Why isn't he with us?
Travelling with the Prince. On a great galleon. It's not fair!

ESMERALDA. Don't be jealous. You know perfectly well that
somebody has to look after the scenery.

WILLIAM (*getting up in his agitation*). But he's only been with
us a week!

MRS CROKE. Oh do sit down, everybody, please sit down –
please –

ESMERALDA. Hey – whoops – breakers ahead – rocks and
reefs and terrible cliffs – turn the boat round – out to – sea
quick –

MRS CROKE. Too late – we're going over –

They all give a great cry as they are spilt out into the surf.

After an interval of disastrous confusion they all struggle ashore.

CROKE. Where are we?

WILLIAM. We're on shore.

ESMERALDA. It must be the coast of France.

MRS CROKE. It can't be the coast of France, there ought to be a lighthouse.

WILLIAM. It's a Channel Island – it's Guernsey, it's Jersey – could it possibly be Sark?

MRS CROKE. But there ought to be a lighthouse.

Enter a FRENCH OFFICER.

FRENCH OFFICER. A thousand pardons, *Madame*, but the lighthouse is out of order. We have so recently been at war and it is – how you say – a shortage of oil for the lamp. I am Chief Customs Officer in the service of the King of France – I must ask you all, at once, please – to come up with me to my office and to bring your baggage if you have any and your keys to open it up. Your boat, I much regret, is destroyed to smithereens.

CROKE. But it can't be – it's not ours. It belongs to the King of England.

FRENCH OFFICER. Indeed? How most interesting. Shall we discuss it in the office? Follow me – if you please.

They go off.
The CONSTABLE *then comes on rowing after them. He is wearing oilskins and sou-wester.*

CONSTABLE (*sings*).
    'Fifty guineas is the prize he gave me
    Fifty guineas is the prize I seek
    This wretched tub warn't worth that money
    But I'll get to France if it takes me a week.'
Never would I have agreed to this job if I'd known what

was involved. Where's the British Navy, I'd like to know, lounging and boozing in the saloon bars of Portsmouth, idle, ignorant bell-bottomed layabouts – they ought to send *them* out when it's a question of overseas duty – over seas is the word an' all – over seas over, and into my boat – I've never seen such waves – wow, there's a whopper – watch it, watch it, wait a minute, can't you, I've lost me starboard oar – ow, help, murder, I'm drowning, catastrophe, help – police!

He too is wrecked and scrambles ashore exhausted. The FRENCH OFFICER *re-enters.*

FRENCH OFFICER. French Police and Customs. Will you come up to the office at once, please, and bring your baggage with you.

CONSTABLE. Hey, what about my boat? It cost me fifty guineas.

FRENCH OFFICER. *Vraiment?* And who gave it you? The King of England, *hein?*

CONSTABLE. Gave me what? The boat? The money? What?

FRENCH OFFICER. We'll find out. So come along then – *vite, vite, venez!*

They go off.

The FRENCH OFFICER *re-enters and arranges the stage to establish an office divided into two sections. The* CONSTABLE *is led into one room, the* ACTORS *into the other. The* FRENCH OFFICER *joins the latter. The* ACTORS, *like the* CONSTABLE, *are all wearing sou-westers, and from where he is he cannot see their faces.*

FRENCH OFFICER. I am sorry, *Messieurs, Mesdames,* but I cannot accept your account. You tell to me first, your ship belongs to the King of England, you tell to me after, you have lost all your passports. With the King of England we have just had a most serious war. We do not therefore regard the King of England as a trustworthy person. It is in my opinion you are spies, if not assassins.

CONSTABLE (*peering at them*). One two three four five –
something's gone wrong. There ought to be six. At least I've
caught up with 'em. I must make sure I don't lose touch.

CROKE. I thought I had made it clear, sir, that we are a company of actors. Do we look like assassins?

FRENCH OFFICER. You would be very poor assassins indeed
if you did. How do I know but that the King of England does
not wish to murder the Princess of France? Then there
would be no marriage. Then the war will start again. And
this time, so he hopes, the English will win. You are under
arrest, until you prove your identity. Actors indeed . . .
Nom d'un nom d'un nom d'un cochon! . . .
(*He goes through into the next room.*)
As for you, you also have no passport, is it not?

CONSTABLE. No it's not! It so happens that I have . . . sh-
ssh, this is private . . . do you see what's been wrote in it?

FRENCH OFFICER. Agent of Police? You are the King of
England's police? And you intend to do – what? In the
King of France's boundaries?

CONSTABLE. Yes, well, now – that's a question. International
delicacies, fragilities, andcetera – what on earth am I to say?
I've got it. Security Duties.

FRENCH OFFICER. Security Duties? To protect the Prince of
England in case that some French man should desire to
assassinate and thereby begin the war again?

CONSTABLE. Very forcibly put. That's precisely the –

FRENCH OFFICER. It is an insult to France to suggest that she
does not know how to protect her own guests. *Monsieur
Jacques?*

A VOICE (*offstage*). *Monsieur François?*

FRENCH OFFICER (*calling*). This gentleman is here to look
after the security of the Prince of England. Will you please
ensure that his own security is properly taken care of. *En
prison, s'il vous plaît!*

VOICE. *Bien sûr, Monsieur François.*

FRENCH OFFICER. So go with the Officer who is awaiting you
in there. Go quickly – he will attend to you. *Allez, allez –
vite!*
(*The* CONSTABLE, *puzzled, goes out.*)
And that will do very well for *him* until the wedding is
properly finished. *Allo allo* – what noise is this?

The FRENCH OFFICER *returns to the* ACTORS. *Enter* LUKE
with the FRENCH ACTOR *and* ACTRESS.

FRENCH ACTRESS. *C'est absolument ridicule.*
FRENCH ACTOR. *Je vous assure, monsieur, que tous les artistes
français détestent l'orgueil épouvantable de ces fonctionnaires.
Eh bien, Monsieur le Capitaine, où sont les comédiens anglais?*
ACTORS. Luke! Thank heavens you are here – (*etc.*)
LUKE. Is everyone all right – they've not been mistreating you –
are you all right, Esmeralda – Mrs Croke?
FRENCH OFFICER. *Les comédiens? O là là*, then they are really
indeed comedians? But they have no passports, *Monsieur*,
what else was I to do? *Eh bien*, you are now vouched for by
two of the most celebrated members of the Royal Theatre in
Paris – if indeed, you know them personally, *Monsieur?*
FRENCH ACTOR. They are identified, *Monsieur le Capitaine*, by
this other English actor who has travelled with the Prince.
FRENCH OFFICER. Then it is with great pleasure, *Messieurs,
Mesdames*, that I bid you welcome to France, to our beautiful
France, and may you all enjoy your visit. You accompany
them to Paris, *chère Madame?*
FRENCH ACTRESS. There are coaches prepared at the hotel in
Calais. If you will all walk with me. Ah, how delightful it is
for brother and sister artists to meet together in such amity
after so cruel and so prolonged a period of war! Is it not that
the only true temple of peace and goodwill amongst man-
kind is nothing but the theatre . . .?

She leads them all out.

The FRENCH OFFICER *remains and readjusts the stage. He addresses the audience:*

FRENCH OFFICER.

> We officers who serve the resplendent King of France
> In our so efficient loyalty we leave not a thing to chance.
> Therefore it is most necessary that, fast as they travel,
> To be with His Majesty when they come and to guard his royal safety
> Is the act of a wise man, neither rash, my lords, nor hasty.
> But, at a time of delectable festivity,
> It is not well to put on any front of hostility.
> As a decorous and subservient gentleman of the Court
> I attend my gracious master and I make my report.

(*The* KING OF FRANCE *enters, with great solemnity, with the* PRINCESS *on his arm.*)
Monseigneur!

The OFFICER *presents a chair for the* KING, *who very slowly sits down and extends his leg. The* OFFICER *places a footstool under this.*
The OFFICER *then places a cushion on the floor beside the footstool. The* KING *raps on the floor with his long cane, and the* PRINCESS *sits demurely upon the cushion. The* OFFICER *backs away a little and waits for the* KING *to speak.*

KING OF FRANCE. In fifteen minutes, *Monsieur*, we shall receive the Prince of England. He has arrived? He is correctly attended?

FRENCH OFFICER. *Monseigneur*, with the utmost respect and attention to protocol.

KING OF FRANCE. *Bien.* Before we have the happiness to receive this young man who is to be greatly honoured by the hand of our beloved daughter, we wish to be assured that all is prepared for the entertainments tonight. Tomorrow morning in the cathedral the marriage will be solemnized and immediately afterwards we must bid our child *adieu*. Therefore it is most necessary that her last night in France should be an occasion of artistry and joy. Does the Prince bring with him his troupe of English actors? Shall they contest with our own favourites of the stage for the prize of one hundred guineas?

FRENCH OFFICER. *Oui, Monseigneur* – the actors are in Paris. They have been escorted hither according to instruction by *Monsieur* Hercule and *Madame* Zénobie of the Royal French Theatre.

KING OF FRANCE. Ah, the ravishing *Madame* Zénobie! We have ever a tenderness for *Madame* Zénobie. We shall be pleased to speak with the actors at once.

FRENCH OFFICER. At once, *Monseigneur*. Admit the actors to His Majesty!

The ACTORS, *English and French, all enter and make their bows.*

KING OF FRANCE. *Madame* Zénobie, we are enchanted yet once more by the rare renewed pleasure of kissing your delicate hand.

(*The* KING *has actually risen to receive the* FRENCH ACTRESS *and he prevents her curtsy with a more than courteous kiss.*)

Indeed, *Madame*, you will permit us to kiss your delicate lips . . . Indeed, *Madame* – but no – this is not the proper time – upon a later occasion –*sans doute?*

FRENCH ACTRESS. *Sans doute, cher Monseigneur.*

The KING *now holds out his own hand for the* FRENCH ACTOR *to kiss.*

KING OF FRANCE. *Monsieur* Hercule – you may make your presentations.

FRENCH ACTOR. *Monseigneur*, I am most privileged to present to you, first *Monsieur* Crock, leading tragedian to

His Majesty of England. (Kiss his Majesty's hand, *Monsieur* Crock.) *Madame* Crock, who shall play the leading female roles.

KING OF FRANCE. *Chère Madame*, permit *me*.

He kisses her hand, but without undue familiarity.

FRENCH ACTOR. *Monsieur* Villiaume, *le jeune premier: Mademoiselle* Esmeralda, *soubrette*.

ESMERALDA. Sub-what?

FRENCH OFFICER. Ssh-sh-sh . . .

KING OF FRANCE. *Mademoiselle:* such beauty we had not believed out of England was to be possible.

(*He kisses her hand and rolls his eyes at her. She rolls hers back, which is clearly not the right thing to do. The* KING *freezes a little.*)

Enchanté, Mademoiselle. Now, *Monsieur* Hercule, *Monsieur* Crock, do you have the playbills for your entertainments tonight? May we be privileged to be informed what masterpieces are in store?

CROKE *and the* FRENCH ACTOR *hand playbills to the* OFFICER, *who reads out the titles.*

FRENCH OFFICER. *King Arthur.*

KING OF FRANCE. Very good. A story of chivalry. We shall expect it with keen delight.

FRENCH OFFICER. But what is this, *Monsieur* Hercule? *The tragedy of King Saul and David the Shepherd Boy?*

KING OF FRANCE. How an anointed King went mad and was succeeded by a young man of no account whatever?

FRENCH ACTOR. *Monseigneur*, it is a story from Holy Scripture.

KING OF FRANCE. There are many things in Holy Scripture unsuitable for public performance. You must alter the plot.

FRENCH ACTRESS. But how, *Monseigneur?* The poet who wrote the play is dead.

FRENCH OFFICER. Then you are to find another poet.

KING OF FRANCE. And what part is assigned to you, *chère Madame?*

FRENCH ACTRESS. I am to play the Witch of Endor, *Monseigneur*.

KING OF FRANCE. Oh no, you are to play a beautiful queen. Our favourite actress cannot possibly appear as an old and hideous witch, if she expects to earn for her company the hundred guineas we have promised.

FRENCH OFFICER. Have you the script of the play?

FRENCH ACTOR. It is here, *Monseigneur*.

KING OF FRANCE (*taking the manuscript*). We will rewrite it ourselves. Directly. You need then have no doubts of the correctitude of your portrayal of royalty. And the talents of *Madame* Zénobie will receive their best expression.

LUKE. That sounds remarkably like sharp practice to me.

KING OF FRANCE. Did somebody speak? There is a man in this room whom we have not yet observed. Who is he, and why is he here?

FRENCH ACTOR. Oh but yes, *Monseigneur* – a thousand pardons, *Monseigneur* –

CROKE. It is a terrible error, milord, yes – it appears –

LUKE. It appears I was forgotten. I was lining up at the back of the queue: but by some strange mischance I was totally invisible. Notwithstanding: I'm still here.

FRENCH ACTOR. This – gentleman, *Monseigneur*, is the English – Stage Manager.

KING OF FRANCE. Oh. But he is not an actor. He is a mechanical – a workman – he should not be here at all.

CROKE. Oh, Your Majesty, I do apologize, it is altogether my fault –

ESMERALDA. Well, I'm not apologizing. He's a perfect right to be here. If it hadn't been for him we'd never have got to Paris in the first place.

KING OF FRANCE. *Mademoiselle* – are you by chance a Democrat?

ESMERALDA. No I'm not, I'm a perfectly respectable professional. We've brought our own play with us and we're
going to do it as it's written – if you don't like it, you must
lump it. The King of England liked it and what's good
enough for him – well, I suppose *he* could have written a
better part for me if he'd wanted to – *I* wouldn't have
objected – but it never occurred to him. He led us to believe
it was a fair competition and so it ought to be – if it's not,
we'll go home, and I don't give a –

(*She is surrounded by everyone in a furious panic, compelling her
to be quiet. Her voice tails away, indignantly protesting to the*
CROKES.)

Well, I saw him kissing that French biddy over there all the
way up her arm, even if you didn't and you needn't tell
me . . .

KING OF FRANCE. No matter, she is English. Her ignorance is
excused. But as for this man, we do not like his tone of
voice.

He looks at LUKE.

LUKE. If you're expecting an apology, you're welcome, I am
sure. I don't want to be the man as fouls up the whole issue.
It's *my* bread and butter, you know, as well as these others.

KING OF FRANCE. This is altogether too extra-ordinary. We
do not understand it – we should prefer to forget it. *Monsieur*
Hercule, perhaps you will be so good as to conduct the
English actors out of our presence and – ah – shew to them
the beautiful pictures to our art-gallery or something, until
it is time to prepare for the entertainments. I suppose they
are aware of what an art-gallery is for? They will not smoke
cigars, or write their names upon the paintings? *Alors*, we
are happy to make your acquaintance, *Messieurs*, *Mesdames*.

(*The* FRENCH ACTORS *take the* ENGLISH ACTORS *out.*)

And now, my dear child, we must receive your fiancé:
must we not, my poor fledgling? Before he makes his entry

there are one or two small things it were as well that I should tell you. *Monsieur le Capitaine* – you may bring hither the Prince to our presence.

FRENCH OFFICERS. *Tout à l'heure, Monseigneur.*

Exit the FRENCH OFFICER.

KING OF FRANCE. First then, you must not permit yourself to fall in love with this young man. This marriage is a marriage of politics, not affection. It is not at all impossible that a divorce or separation, within two years or three years, may have to take place. Once England and France recommence their war together, there will be no place for tender sentiment. Do I make myself clear ?

PRINCESS. But only too clear, *mon père, hélas, hélas* . . .

KING OF FRANCE. *Hélas, ma chérie* . . . but such is this cruel world . . . However, you will treat the young Prince with all the courtesy and gentle deference with which you have been embued. He is not, I am informed, altogether unpleasant. Had he been, I would never have given my consent to this wedding. Aha. I hear him come !

(*The* PRINCE *enters, attended by the* FRENCH OFFICER. *Advancing to embrace him*). Aha, my dear son, for so I must call you now. You take from our arms the sweetest treasure of our kingdom. Behold her. She is there. Do not make your reverences to me, my good young man – but make them to your wife.

(*He stands back and admires the* PRINCE *and* PRINCESS. *She rises from her cushion and he bows to kiss her hand. All very grave and tender. The* KING *dismisses the* FRENCH OFFICER *with a gesture of his stick.*)

Speak to her, my son. Give praise to her for her beauty. Our ladies of France expect their gentlemen to excel in poetic devotion. No doubt in England also this will be the custom – no ?

PRINCE.

>It is a custom that we have learnt from your excellent example.
>
>*Mademoiselle*, if I were to offer to compare the whiteness of your temple
>
>As it shews beneath the dark curl of your hair, above the ear,
>
>To the gleaming egg-shells of the Bird of Paradise as they lie in their nest,
>
>Half-concealed by the soft feathers of their mother's trembling breast –
>
>Would you then condemn me for impertinence? I do fear
>
>That my tongue is too forward for true courtesy:
>
>And yet it is compelled by the unprecedented mystery
>
>That lies within your eyes. Your deep eyes, and your smile,
>
>Are they both an expression of the profundity of your soul?
>
>If they are, then I am happy and for all my livelong days
>
>My voice shall continue to proclaim my love and your praise.

KING OF FRANCE. Quite exquisite. You are well instructed. Now daughter – your reply?

PRINCESS.

>Sir, the beauty that you claim to see in me
>
>If it exists at all, is but the surface of my nature.
>
>What lies beneath it must be revealed in the future:
>
>I am certain that by reason of your love I shall find myself so free
>
>As to shew you myself utterly without any concealment:
>
>And I trust that you will then find no cause for disappointment.

KING OF FRANCE. Perfect – upon both sides. So, my dear children, it is appropriate, is it not, that I leave you both together. You will have so much to say to one another, in private, as is only fitting, after all, when one is young, and in love.

He takes his departure.
The PRINCE *and* PRINCESS *look at one another.*

PRINCE.
Because of England I must marry you.
Because of the instructions of my father.

PRINCESS.
Indeed indeed I would far rather
That I should marry you because of what you are
Than marry you because of France.
Your hands are thick and red
They would cut meat as well as bread
You have upon your shoulders a strong round head
Would thrust itself into a wall and break the bricks
    and mortar down:
Your body is the body of a hod-carrying clown
And yet you speak in sweet words like the son of a
    true king.
This is to combine the earth and the fire
In a way that we in France do not look for – nor
    desire –
Unless, like myself, we are lovers of all things strange.
Englishman, rude, wild and strange, range
Your arms round me. We wed for no affection
But for politics only. Such is the instruction.
Yet why should we not enjoy it while we can?

PRINCE (*a little embarrassed but touched by the fervour of her embrace*).
Mademoiselle, I am a careful and obedient young man.
When my father says 'Remember

The fate of nations is in danger'
It behoves me to mark his words and write them in
    my heart.
I intend to continue as I swore that I would start:
I must not fall in love. Neither must you.
Nevertheless one flesh must be made out of our two
(By the blessing of the Church): and by the blessing
    of good luck
Yours and no-one else's is the fruit that I must pluck.
Therefore, as I cram its fragrant pulp between my teeth
Let me not pause for a moment's heedful breath –
Let me tell myself rather 'Between this instant and my
    death
There can be no pleasure equal to what I now feel.
Let me not scatter peel nor pip nor core
Upon the ground to remind me that I could have
    eaten yet more.'
I shall swallow you whole
If only for a while:
Let us both tell our children
That we ate and we were full.

He picks her up in his arms and runs out with her.
Enter the FRENCH OFFICER *and the* FRENCH ACTORS.

FRENCH OFFICER. The order for the entertainments this
evening is as follows. His Majesty and Their Royal Highnesses are to dine at six o'clock. As soon as the tables have
been cleared away, you, *Monsieur* Hercule, will present the
French play upon the floorboards of the dining hall. You
have acted there many times, you will be familiar with the
arrangements. Have your scenery in the Kitchen passages
ready to be set up. There are no problems, no? *Eh bien* – we
continue –

He makes as though to lead them out, but they do not follow.

FRENCH ACTOR. Problems, *Monsieur le Capitaine* – *sacré nom de Dieu*, but we have multitudes of problems!

FRENCH OFFICER. *Eh, quoi, par exemple?*

FRENCH ACTOR. *Eh, quoi?* Consider this. We have rehearsed at great trouble and with enormous expenditure of money and of time and of our vital resources – we have made it without question a matter of certainty that the work we present before the King and his daughter and her husband shall be of the most excellent quality that it is possible for us to shew. And at the last moment – the last conceivable moment, *Monsieur* – we are told it will not do! His Majesty, if you please, must find in our poor text some sentiments of subversion, republicanism, revolution, I know not what – indeed we are honoured he must rewrite it himself – but how long will it take, and how is it possible that we can learn the lines by heart? And as for *Madame* –

FRENCH ACTRESS. As for *Madame* – *bonté de bon Dieu!* – a completely new role, *Monsieur le Capitaine*, not even yet written, and my costumes already found and my make-up prepared – *oh là là là, c'est terrible, épouvantable* – *oh rage, oh désespoir!*

FRENCH OFFICER. I fancy, *Madame*, that it were better you should reserve these emotional transports for the occasion of the play. To console you, I will remind you that His Majesty has a great dislike for prolonged entertainment. Therefore such portions of your play that you cannot remember you can easily omit – provided that you do not omit any lines that the King himself has written. Will that make it more easy?

FRENCH ACTOR. *Mais non, Monsieur*, it will not! For it is only the lines of the King that we are likely to forget.

FRENCH ACTOR ⎫ *Entrailles du Pape*, but our reputation
FRENCH ACTRESS ⎭ from this day is entirely destroyed!

FRENCH OFFICER. No no, you are extreme. I cannot talk to you when you behave in this manner. I must go and see the

English actors and apprise them of their arrangements.
Where are they – in the gallery ?

FRENCH ACTOR. *Je ne sais pas.* I last saw them looking for a
cup of tea in the Privy Council ante-chamber – ridiculous,
barbarous . . .

(*The* OFFICER *goes out.*)

Their own reputation is already more destroyed than ours.
That is at any rate one thing we can be glad about.

FRENCH ACTRESS. But is it, *mon cher ?* Such ruffians, such
rude peasants as are these English – is it not possible that the
King will take such pleasure in their uncouth foreign ways,
at the same time that he is *dis*pleased because we have forgot
our parts, that in the end he will give to them the hundred
guineas and we shall be for ever disgraced before all France ?
Do you not realize it is necessary for the King to flatter the
English, by reason of the peace treaty ?

FRENCH ACTOR. If only we could know how good they were
going to be. Surely they cannot be any good at all, when their
manners are so gross ? But yet perhaps they can – is there not
a way we can find to make them so utterly ridiculous upon
the stage that the King cannot for very shame award to them
the prize ? Could we not, for example, contrive to make them
drunk ?

FRENCH ACTRESS. It is not probable. They are, after all,
professionals. I do not believe they will let themselves get
drunk.

FRENCH ACTOR. I am afraid that that is true. What, then, do
you suggest ?

FRENCH ACTRESS. A cup of tea. They cried for tea. They are
hungry, *n'est-ce pas ?* For the English, remember, tea is more
than a drink, it is a great plate of bread and butter, with
bacon and egg, and – now, supposing they were to be given
their great plate – and in with the egg and the bacon and the
beefsteak and the rest of it, there were to be a little something, a *soupçon*, that is all, which would make them feel so

queer that when they come to act, they – *oh là, là* – do you not see it – *mon Dieu,* it would be catastrophe!

FRENCH ACTOR. Be silent – here they come . . .

They both retire to the back of the stage as the FRENCH OFFICER *brings in the* ENGLISH ACTORS.

FRENCH OFFICER. At seven o'clock, *Monsieur* Crock, the French play will commence in the dining hall – it will conclude, I suppose, at about a quarter past eight – the King does not wish to endure delay between the pieces, so it has been decided that you will act in this room here. While your French colleagues are performing, you will have time to make yourselves ready: His Majesty and their Royal Highnesses will move from one room to the other and you will start directly they take their seats in here – twenty minutes past eight. You understand? Are there any questions? No? Then I will leave you.

ESMERALDA. Wait a minute – grub?

FRENCH OFFICER. *Pardon?*

ESMERALDA. I said grub – nosh – din-dins – you know – eggo, soupo – fisho –

CROKE. The fact is, sir, we *are* hungry, and we wondered if any arrangement –

FRENCH OFFICER. That, *Monsieur,* I regret, is not part of my function.

The FRENCH OFFICER *goes out.*

WILLIAM (*reading a piece of paper over to himself*). We, the undersigned, being members of His Britannic Majesty's Company of Players, at present on tour in France, desire to protest against –

CROKE. What on earth do you think you're doing? We must get ready for the play. Come along now, Luke – where are you, Luke, set the stage up at once, we have very little time.

WILLIAM. I am composing a formal protest, Mr Croke. The

French King himself is writing the play for his own actors to appear in. Clearly the prize has been awarded in advance. It is absolutely monstrous.

LUKE *and* ESMERALDA *start to erect the stage.*

CROKE. You are quite right. It *is* monstrous. But really, William, you should know better than to make a public quarrel about it. We must endure these political intrigues for I am sure it is political – with professional equanimity. Let us all make certain – all of us, my dears – that our own work, at any rate, should be beyond reproach – and keep these disruptive protests for a later date. When we get home to London would be the best time to make complaints. It is most unprofessional to start off with such ill-feeling.

MRS CROKE. But a protest in London, Antonius, will not bring back the hundred guineas.

CROKE. Nor will a protest in Paris, my dear – I can assure you of that.

MRS CROKE. At least they might have offered us something to eat. I saw the French actors quite distinctly sitting down to bowls of soup and glasses of wine – when I attempted to join them some sort of butler informed me that all the tables were reserved. We are very definitely being treated – from the beginning – as inferiors – and I feel it very deeply.

The FRENCH ACTOR *comes forward.*

FRENCH ACTOR. *Madame*, you do mistake. There was no intention whatever to deprive you of your tea. The servant was under an unfortunate misapprehension. I myself shall take order that a meal be brought in to you. You may eat while you prepare your play.

MRS CROKE. Oh well, that is *quite* different – we are really most grateful – thank you so much, Mister.

FRENCH ACTRESS. *Madame*, it is an honour to render service to fellow-artists. *Bon appétit !*

FRENCH ACTOR. *Bon appétit !*

The FRENCH ACTORS *go out.*

MRS CROKE. How very charming the French can be – can they
not, my dears ?

LUKE. When they set themselves out to it. You haven't seen
'em dealing with their prisoners of war.

CROKE. Luke, that will do. The war is now over: and nobody
here desires to be reminded of it. Most tactless, my dear
fellow – please recollect yourself.

LUKE. Whatever you say, Mr Croke – you're the gaffer – we're
just the workmen and mechanicals – aren't we, Esmeralda–
we don't exist – we're disgusting, we have a bad smell – we
should never have been brought!

CROKE. That is quite enough of that. You have caused sufficient trouble already today. Please remember your place and
do the work that you are paid for.

LUKE. I am doing it. Very briskly. I am neither clamouring for
food nor composing impotent protests. Esmeralda is assisting
me. With her usual incompetent charm: but at least she's
stuck into it. I observe nobody else is. Right then: Act One.
You want the rose-trellis up.

WILLIAM. It's not needed until much later.

LUKE. But you want it in position. Anything else! What about
the big box ? For Merlin's magic. Do we have it in the first
act, or don't we ? There was some dispute in London.

CROKE. We decided to have it. So bring it on, please – don't
waste time. I would like to run through again just the first
few lines of the very first scene. Remember the situation.

Mordred has sent the King a poisoned apple with a letter
pretending that it has come from Sir Lancelot. William, you
enter, eating the apple – you are feeling exceedingly ill, you
complain about it to the Queen. So do it, will you – carry
on.

WILLIAM. 'I feel a strange disturbance in my bowels . . .'

CROKE. Exactly! I thought that was the line. 'Bowels' will have to come out.

WILLIAM. Why?

CROKE. You ought to know why. It should have become evident to you today that one thing the French cannot abide is vulgarity. 'Bowels' will have to come out.

WILLIAM. Then what am I to say?

CROKE. What about heart?

WILLIAM. But a poisoned piece of apple wouldn't lodge in my heart.

ESMERALDA. It goes past it on the way down – it might have stopped there for a bit of a kickback, mightn't it?

She gives a belch.

MRS CROKE. No, it might not – that, Esmeralda, is – if any-thing – an even more vulgar idea.

CROKE. Quiet, quiet, I am turning it over in my mind – here we are – 'I feel a strange disturbance – I am ill!'

MRS CROKE. One moment, Antonius, I think they are bringing us our tea.

CROKE. Ah, tea, tea – tea – splendid, we shall all feel much better and be able in a few moments to return to our work refreshed . . .

Enter a COOK *(if possible, a procession of* COOKS*) bearing silver dishes with great dish-covers.*

COOK. *Monsieur,* it is the order of His Majesty that these few trifling refreshments should be provided for your company.

The FRENCH ACTOR *and* ACTRESS *have come in behind the* COOK.

CROKE. This is really too good – shall we assemble ourselves here – if you will put the dishes down upon this box –
(*While the* ACTORS *are getting into position, the* FRENCH ACTRESS *distracts the* COOK'S *attention for a moment by*

flashing her great fan across his face. She apologizes charmingly,
and while he is smiling an acknowledgement to her, the FRENCH
ACTOR *whips away the dish-cover and sprinkles poison in the*
food.)
We are most grateful to the King – I mean, my compliments
to His Majesty – I mean – er – yes, well, most kind of him to
think of us. And thank *you.*

COOK (*accepting a tip with disdain*). Zut, alors, Messieurs,
Mesdames . . .

The COOK *and* FRENCH ACTORS *withdraw again with bows.*

CROKE. Now: we're not holding up the rehearsal just to sit here
and guzzle – here's a plate for each of you – and we'll get on
with the work while we eat. Hello – he's only sent four.

LUKE. That's right. I'm not here.

MRS CROKE. Oh but Mr Luke, I'm sure there's some mistake –

LUKE. Oh no there's not. But I'm not daft, I took precautions.

LUKE *takes out a packet of sandwiches and starts to eat as he*
works.

WILLIAM. Where did you get those?

LUKE. While you lot were in the picture-gallery, I went out and
found a café. They have them, you know, in Paris – they've
got tables, on the pavement.

ESMERALDA. But it's not fair that he shouldn't have any of
this – it smells beautiful – what is it? Garlic or something –
I'm not going to eat if Luke's not going to eat.

LUKE. I am eating. For God's sake carry on and stop trying to
be compassionate.

ESMERALDA. No no, you must have mine. I don't want it –
take it away.

MRS CROKE. There is no need to sulk, Esmeralda – if you do
not want your portion there are others here who would be
glad of it.

She picks up ESMERALDA'S *dish.*

ESMERALDA. Oh, but I didn't mean –

MRS CROKE.

> Didn't mean but had to say it
> Took the bill and couldn't pay it.

You'll know better in future, my dear, to make boasts you
can't fulfil.

She begins to eat from ESMERALDA'S *dish.* ESMERALDA –
*angry – gets round behind her, touches her on the left shoulder,
when she turns her head to the left,* ESMERALDA *snatches some
food from the right of the dish.* MRS CROKE *catches her at it and
gives her a slap, but she is too late to prevent her swallowing a
mouthful, in triumph.*

LUKE. Oh, leave it alone then, and fill up with these.

He gives ESMERALDA *a sandwich.*

CROKE. Our behaviour is deteriorating. You do not appear to
realize – *any* of you – that in a very short while we shall be in
front of an audience. And a great deal depends upon it. We
haven't even sorted out that first line of yours, William!
Get upon the stage at once and we will begin from where we
left off.

> 'I feel a strange disturbance – I am ill.'

And then will you give me the rest of the speech – I seem to
remember there are other intestinal references that may have
to be altered. Carry on, please – and no more foolery.

WILLIAM.

> I feel a strange disturbance – I am ill.
> Can I have eaten something I should not?
> Can I have –

CROKE. No no no – where is the dignity and the royalty of this
part? You seem to have forgotten everything we have rehearsed! What's the matter? Are you ill?

WILLIAM. Of course I'm ill – I've just said so, haven't I?

CROKE. I don't mean in the play. I mean in fact. Are you ill, boy, or what's wrong with you?

WILLIAM. I don't exactly know. What about you?

CROKE. What about me? I am always ill. It is idiots like you that make me ill. Good lord, boy, I remember playing Alexander the Great before an audience of drunken coalheavers when I had a temperature of a hundred and six! And they gave me the longest round of applause at the end of it that I ever remember in the whole of my career! I spent six weeks in bed after that experience and the doctors all said they had seen nothing like it – didn't they, my dear?

MRS CROKE. Oh, don't talk about it, Antonius, the very thought of it brings me out in – in – oh dear, what *is* the matter with me? I shall faint if I have to stand here any longer.

There is a sound of trumpets offstage – and applause.

CROKE. Oh good lord, it must be later than we thought. There is the French play starting already . . . Are any of us fit enough to go on tonight – at all? Whatever is the matter with this company?

LUKE. There's nothing the matter with me.

CROKE. I think we are all suffering from exhaustion after the hardships of the journey, or something – perhaps we should all go and rest for an hour. Yes, yes, a good rest, get our feet up, lie down . . . Luke, if you are sure you are feeling fit, you had better hold the fort here – see that everything is quite ready . . . and – er – don't forget to give us a call in plenty of time to begin . . . oh dear me, I am so giddy . . .

He staggers off, followed by MRS CROKE, WILLIAM *and the* CLOWN, *all more or less incapacitated.*

LUKE. You know what's wrong with them, don't you – ?

ESMERALDA. No. What is wrong with them? They're not used to eating snails, I suppose, but neither am I and I did have quite a mouthful –

LUKE. Yes, I know you did, and you'd best watch out, dear –
or you will be going the same way. Why, it's obvious what's
happened. Those Froggy so-and-sos have hocussed the grub.

ESMERALDA. Hocussed it?

LUKE. Alright, then, poisoned it – though I doubt if they'd have
the guts to run so far as murder. More likely just enough to
make everyone sick. It's a real old French trick – you know –
we had a half-a-company of pikemen laid out flat on their
backs once with galloping diarrhoea after eating their break-
fasts in a little village alehouse just short of the Belgian
border. If they'd stoop to it in wartime, when there's supposed
to be international rules of conduct, they aren't very likely to
have any scruples with artistic prestige in question. It's a pity,
really, isn't it, that *we* didn't think of it first?

ESMERALDA. So what are we going to do?

LUKE. Ah, it may be a false alarm. It could be just they're
over-tired like the old fellow says. We'd better carry on and
make sure it's all ready, and then if they're still incapable,
we'll have to call the whole show off.

ESMERALDA. But we can't do that, Luke – what about the
hundred guineas?

LUKE. You weren't counting on that – were you? Not here –
not in Paris, with the leading lady of the Frog actors being
the sweetheart of the King? Why, we never had the chance
of a pig-in-the-shambles of winning that there prize, so don't
deceive yourself. Now look here, are you certain that you
aren't feeling off it? I don't give a damn over the state of old
Croke's stomach but I'd hate to see *you* going down in a
convulsion.

ESMERALDA. I have no intention whatever of going down in a
convulsion, so stop trying to be compassionate.

LUKE. Who's trying to be compassionate? What I said, I said
on purpose. I said –

ESMERALDA. Luke, we've got to *do* something! Find a doctor,
find an antidote –

LUKE. No no no, use your sense, girl – Frog doctors – Frog poisons? Ah, not at all, nobody's dead. And they're not going to be neither. Let nature take her course: and serve 'em right for being so greedy. But you, you weren't greedy. Yet you did eat something. So how are you? Tell the truth then. I'm asking *you*.

ESMERALDA. I'm all right. At the moment . . . Well, more or less . . . Yes. Now *I'm* asking *you*. I'm not bothered about Flanders. But what about Ireland?

LUKE. Ireland? I'm not with you.

ESMERALDA. You're not with her either. But are you inclined to go back?

LUKE. Ah, ah – the penny drops! Ireland. You mean that wife?

ESMERALDA. She still *is* your wife?

LUKE. Oh God – the truth to tell you, she never was, she never was . . .

> The product of a rainy day
> Upon the shores of Galway Bay –
> A little cottage with a smoky fire,
> The old man gone, to sell his piglets at the fair,
> His daughter left behind, so agreeable and kind
> To the drunken trooper knocking rat-tat-tat upon the door –
> Half an hour of bright desire
> In the middle of a war.

I don't know why I bothered to remember it, even. There's nothing about *you* to remind me of it at all.

They kiss. Then ESMERALDA *breaks away.*

ESMERALDA. Except the half hour.

LUKE. Eh, what? I'm not with you . . .?

ESMERALDA. No, I know you're not. You're a vagrant. You've no loyalty nor anything. The whole company's in trouble, and the play's ruined and you don't care! Where are you going?

LUKE.

> My travelling expenses are not yet all spent.
> I am going back to the café
> Where I am perfectly happy
> To sit down in content
> On my own, all alone,
> And drink a bottle of wine.
> Nothing that you have
> Has anything to do,
> As far as I can see,
> With anything of mine.

Good-bye . . .

He makes to leave.

ESMERALDA. Oh, wait a minute, you silly man – I didn't mean –

LUKE.

> Didn't mean but had to say it
> Took the bill and couldn't pay it.

Heard that before somewhere, haven't we, this afternoon?

He goes out.

ESMERALDA. And now he's gone. Well, I'm not going to let him sit all alone in the café – he's quite ridiculous to be so touchy.

> I shall go after him and follow him
> And if necessary I shall marry him:
> A single man of his age and attainments
> Has no right to lay claim to such proud independence.

She goes out after him.
She immediately returns.

But I can't go – and neither can he – we can't leave the stage and all our props like this – oh why not, anyway – there isn't going to be a play and even if there is who on earth will want to steal any of this old lumber . . . wait a minute, here's an Officer – I'll ask him to keep an eye on it.

(*Enter the* CONSTABLE *disguised as a* FRENCH OFFICER.)

Excuse me – I wonder if you would mind looking after our stage until we come back?

CONSTABLE (*recognizing her with alarm, and concealing his face*). Not to speako Anglish – *polly-voo franzey, silver-plate.*

ESMERALDA. Oh dear – *noo: tootersweet: retoorn: sivoo-play: regarday apray no stahge? Sivoo-play?*

CONSTABLE (*anxious to be rid of her*). We – *wee-wee* – wee.

ESMERALDA. Thank you very much – er – *mercy bocoo. Bong swarr.*

CONSTABLE. *We – we-wee* . . .

(*She goes out.*)

Eh, that was a close one. For I am not what I seem. Not bad, though? With the accent and all? *Commong voo portey voo mounseer? Quelle* terrible weather *noos avongs ohjoort-wee!* Of course this disguising business would be a darn sight more pleasurable if it was done with the direct aim of catching the murderer. Instead of which I am forced to conceal myself from my own alleged colleagues – I mean, the French police, who locked me up, no less, in some sort of a fortress. By an intrepid manoeuvre, I managed to knock one of them over the nut and put on his change of raiment. Boldly I set forth, saluting to left and right, until I attained the open country. A discreet use of the lingo, picked ûp during my confinement, enabled me to get to Paris, and by means of quite remarkable effrontery and cheek I obtained entrance into the Royal Palace. So: here I am, and here's the traces of the one I'm after. I don't know where *she's* gone off to – but she didn't recognize me, which is good – and apparently the play has not yet taken place.

(*A burst of laughter and slow handclapping from offstage.*)

Ah – there is already entertainment now proceeding in some other room.

(*Boos and whistles.*)

And not, by the sound of it, particularly successful. Now, when they come to perform in here, I shall – by virtue of my uniform – take a discreet place in the wings and observe what's going on. I shall count the members of the cast, both on and off the stage, and when I have succeeded in making the numbers up to six, I shall then be enabled to eliminate the innocent parties, and in the end identify the miscreant in their midst. Which is good routine police work and just what I'm cut out for.

(*The sounds of audience disapproval offstage reach a crescendo. The* PRINCESS *runs in, smothering hysterical laughter – she flops down on the box and gives way to it in private.*)

Hey-up, here comes one of them. No she's not though – she's a stranger – there was but two women actors with the company and neither of 'em was her – you don't suppose that she could be a *he*? I mean, he has been in the habit of concealing himself very cleverly – I wouldn't put it past him to try to pass off as a woman – it's just what you'd expect when you're dealing with theatricals – no sense of morality or public decency whatever. I'll keep well into the background and observe his behaviour while he thinks he is alone. That is always most indicative.

PRINCESS. *Oh, par ma foi – quelle drôlene fantastique!* It was necessary for me to go away otherwise I should have burst – and for a Princess of France to give way to helpless laughter in the middle of a play would have been so disgraceful – my father would never have forgiven me – never –

(*She laughs again.*)

They forgot – *oh mon Dieu* – they forgot every line my father had written for them, and *Madame* Zénobie whom I cannot abide, she burst into tears in the middle of the stage and she turns to the audience and my father in the middle of it and she curses and swears at us all like a fishwife in the market – and she strikes *Monsieur* Hercule across the face with her

fist and he kicks her in the bottom – *oh, mon Dieu*, I should
not say that word – it is not a good word for a Princess of
France – but he kicks her at any rate where I have wanted for
so many years for to kick her myself – and she falls upon the
stage and all the audience whistle and shout – and there is my
father with a face like the public executioner – he cannot
speak, he is so angry – he will never again, never, speak to
Madame Zénobie – she must earn her living from this day
forth in the cheap workmen's cabarets and the little theatres
of the streets and for that I am so happy – she was an avarici-
ous wicked woman and now thank God is she punished!

CONSTABLE. His demeanour – if it *is* his – is clearly uncon-
trolled, see, he rolls about and gnaws the backs of his hands
as though in the torments of most justified remorse. Now
what I think I'd better do is to creep up behind him and give
him – at what we call the psychological moment – a little
reminder of his crime. Watch me – this is crafty . . .

(*He creeps up behind the* PRINCESS, *sits down with his back to
her, pulls his hat down over his eyes, and speaks in an unexpected high strained voice.*)

> Blood on a bottle and a hole in his head
> But strange to say he was not dead.

PRINCESS (*whipping round*). *Eh, bon Dieu – quoi ?*

CONSTABLE.

> You'd better have buried him where he lay
> Lest he walk and talk on a latter day.

(*He whips round too and seizes her.*)

Right, you're frightened. Pale as death, you give away your
very soul! Take off that wig.

PRINCESS. *Qu'est-ce que c'est que ça ? Un gendarme de mon
père ? Vous m'avez suivi, n'est-ce pas, parce-que le roi mon père
croit que j'aime le prince et je veux qu'il me baise dans une
chambre particulière – mais ce n'est pas vrai – je ne suis pas
fausse et je vous assure, Monsieur –*

CONSTABLE. Jabber jabber jabber – ? You can't deceive me,

you're as English as I am. I said take it off. And we'll have off
that gown and all – I want to see the soldier's coat you wear
beneath it –

Enter PRINCE.

PRINCE. Good God, sir, take your hands off!

He grabs the CONSTABLE *and throws him across the stage.*

CONSTABLE. Ah – an accomplice. So I'll take you in as well.
At least you haven't got the gall to try and talk in French –
why, I could tell this lad's accent a mile away – get on with
yer. Now just wait there while I get my truncheon found –

His disguise hampers him in this operation.

PRINCE. By heaven, you are English.
CONSTABLE. Of course I'm English. And proud of it – with
reason. I'm more than just mere English – upon this soil of
France I am the King of England.
PRINCE. What!
CONSTABLE. Because I am his Law and Order, and in his
unavoidable absence I stand here in his place. It is my duty
to warn you that anything you say –
PRINCE. So you're the King of England. Then who am I?
What's this – upon my head?

He indicates his coronet.

CONSTABLE. Cardboard. You can't fool me. I know a theatri-
cal property when I see one
(*The* PRINCE *has drawn his sword.*)
And don't you threaten me with your old wooden sword.
I've not reached my term of years and experience without
learning summat about masqueraders' ways and means.
(*The* PRINCE *pricks him with the sword.*)
Ow-hey-up, that's sharp! You've got no right to use a real

blade like that upon the stage – it's dangerous, you could hurt someone – ow-ow . . .!

In struggling with the PRINCE *he knocks the latter's coronet off.*

CONSTABLE. Wait a moment, that was a funny noise to be made by just a bit of cardboard . . .

PRINCE. Pick it up.

CONSTABLE. Wait a moment –

PRINCE. Pick it up!

CONSTABLE (*picking it up and weighing it apprehensively in his hands*). Where did you get this ? I mean, please tell me that you stole it – or something like that – I mean – I mean, like, looking at your face, now that I have the opportunity to see you right close-up – I mean, in London, you were –

PRINCE. Yes ?

CONSTABLE. Oh no – you're not the –

PRINCE. Yes.

CONSTABLE. The Prince . . .? I did, I saw you – just a minute, like, in London . . . oh my lord, what have I done ?

PRINCE. You have insulted the lady who is about to be my wife.

CONSTABLE. Oh no – it's all a mistake – like, mistaken identity – it could have happened to anyone –

PRINCE. Yes it could – could it not ? Of course you were not to know the lady's exalted rank. But nevertheless, she is a lady. Perhaps we should inquire of her what ought to be done to you ? *Mademoiselle ?*

PRINCESS. This man has laid his hands upon the daughter of a King – according to the laws of France he should be torn to pieces with red-hot pincers.

PRINCE. Very true, my love, but there's a problem. The laws of France are one thing but the laws of England are another. And according to the laws of England – why, this man *is* the laws of England. In fact, I would go further – I have half a notion that he is supposed to be my bodyguard. If we tear him to pieces, we tear the peace treaty to pieces. We're not supposed to do that – at least, not for a year or two. Therefore I suggest that for the moment we forget about the laws of either country and we forget about being the daughter and the son of a pair of Kings, and we knock him down and beat him up and throw him down the stairs and say no more about him. He, I guarantee, will say no more about us.

PRINCESS. I think that is a very good idea – I will help you to carry it out.

She does so. The CONSTABLE *makes his exit upon all fours, crying for mercy.*

CONSTABLE. Oh mercy, mercy, I didn't mean it – how was I to know that your crown was real gold – Oh! My lord, it looked like cardboard – cardboard, cardboard. . .

The PRINCE *and* PRINCESS *embrace.*
Enter the FRENCH OFFICER.

FRENCH OFFICER. Ah milord, His Majesty in a few moments will expect the English actors to begin. Where are the English actors? Gentlemen – *Monsieur* Crock! You are to start a little earlier! *Monsieur* Crock!

Enter CROKE. *He looks pretty ill.*

CROKE. Hello – oh yes, the Captain – yes . . . What, is it, Captain – please . . .?

FRENCH OFFICER. Are you ready to begin?

CROKE. Oh – oh – oh yes, we are quite ready – yes indeed, we must perform. Oh – oh – oh – William, my dear wife – are you ready – we must perform, my dears.

CROKE *goes out.*

FRENCH OFFICER. But what is wrong with him, milord? Such lethargy, such apathy –

PRINCE. Oh, I expect it's just stage fright. Even the best ones have it, you know. But these chaps are very good, I've seen them in London – they won't let you down.

FRENCH OFFICER. *Eh bien*, I tell His Majesty . . .

The FRENCH OFFICER *goes out.*

PRINCESS. Just one or two more moments we have yet to ourselves.

They embrace again.
Enter LUKE *and* ESMERALDA, *their arms round one another singing.*

LUKE *and* ESMERALDA: (*sing*).
      'When cares and troubles throng about
      Just take a glass of wine
      I've got my arm around your waist
      And you've got yours round mine – '

ESMERALDA *stumbles.*

LUKE. Watch it now – that vinn-rooge is stronger than what it seems –

ESMERALDA. It's nothing to do with the wine, love – I think it's the hocussing starting to work –

LUKE. Oh no! Oh dear – I thought you said you were immune – hello though – we've got company.

PRINCE. I am sorry to disturb your – your carousal, Mr Stage Manager – but I imagine you are wanted backstage. The King will be here directly and the play must begin on time. Now the French actors, I am glad to say, made a very poor impression indeed, we're expecting a great deal from you and for God's sake don't let us down. You have a very good chance of winning the prize.

LUKE. That's all you think. Are they conscious, back in there?

PRINCE. What's the matter? They've not got drunk!

LUKE. Not drunk. They're all ill.

PRINCE. Impossible!

LUKE. I don't tell stories.

PRINCE. All of them? Not all of them? But you two are all right – both of you –

LUKE. One of us.

ESMERALDA. Both of us.

PRINCE. Well, you'll have to act the play yourselves. You'll have to get on there and do *something*.

LUKE. But *I* am not an actor. I'm a proletarian mechanical and I'm strictly non-professional.

PRINCE. But think of England, Mr –

LUKE. Luke.

PRINCE. Mr Luke – think of the national prestige. You have been a soldier, have you not – you have confronted the French upon the field of honour, Mr Luke – then here is your Creçy, your Poitiers, your Agincourt, today – pluck up your spirits, man, remember your country, remember your King!

PRINCESS. Remember, *Monsieur* Luke, the one hundred guineas.

LUKE. Now that's a better argument.

PRINCESS. I would so love to see you win it. You are a strong English roastbeef, just like my dear *fiancé* – I too am now English – go on, and win the prize.

LUKE (*as* PRINCESS *kisses him*). A much better argument – it has a great deal of force.

ESMERALDA. Not as far as I go, madam: but I am a professional and I fully intend to act.

PRINCE (*to* ESMERALDA). Now you're not to be jealous – it is but once in a lifetime he can kiss a real princess. And once in a lifetime that you can kiss a prince.

He starts to kiss ESMERALDA, *but is interrupted by a trumpet.*

PRINCESS. No, no, the King will enter.

PRINCE. If they can act at all back in there, they must do

whatever they can. If not, you must do it for them. Good luck then, and good hunting.

LUKE and ESMERALDA go backstage. The KING of FRANCE makes his entry, the FRENCH OFFICER in attendance.

KING OF FRANCE. We trust that the misfortunes of the earlier part of the evening will be fully redeemed by what we are about to see. *Monsieur le Capitaine*, we are ready, I think. Let the actors commence.

FRENCH OFFICER. *Mais oui, Monseigneur.* The play may now commence! Do you hear me, there? Begin.

Enter WILLIAM as King Arthur, MRS CROKE as Guinevere.

PRINCE (*to the PRINCESS*). Well, thank God, at least there's two of them can walk upon their feet.

PRINCESS. But for how long – ? That is the question . . .

WILLIAM. I feel.

A horrid silence.

KING OF FRANCE. Do not let yourself be embarrassed by the importance of your audience. We lend a gracious ear. Continue.

WILLIAM. I feel . . . I feel – a strange disturbance in my bowels!

KING OF FRANCE (*to the PRINCE*). Bowels? What is the meaning of this – this crudity, *Monsieur* – ?

MRS CROKE. And so do I – Your Majesty, excuse us – if you can –

MRS CROKE subsides into WILLIAM'S arms. He supports her for a moment and then collapses also. They both stagger feebly out.

KING OF FRANCE (*rising*). This – is – not – what – we expected!

LUKE (*behind the scene – very loud and frantic*).
          Of course it's not.
          We've changed the plot.

The King is dead before the play's begun.

(*He enters – he has not changed his clothes, and is wearing Lancelot's mask.*)

Who is to continue?

I alone survive:

King Arthur's eldest son!

KING OF FRANCE. *Oh . . .* pardon our interruption. For one moment, I quite thought –

LUKE.

So did they all.

Poisoners, assassins,

Traitors who to secure their wicked ends

Murdered their sovereign

And his wife

And all his friends.

KING OF FRANCE. But – surely your King Arthur lost his life in a great battle?

PRINCE. Oh yes . . . This isn't him. It's King Arthur the Second. (*Prompting* LUKE.) King Arthur the Second.

KING OF FRANCE. King Arthur the Second? This is most interesting. Well, well, we shall be educated as well as entertained. Continue, continue . . .

LUKE.

So: I am left to rule the land

Alone. The sword is for my hand –

The crown is for my head. I wear –

(*He turns his coat red side out again. He picks up William's sword, and crown.*)

– The blood-red garb of royalty and I swear

To seek those villains out to the world's end who would dare

Destroy my father and my mother –

What's more they've gone and killed my brother –

(*He turns and looks backstage and calls.*)

What? . . . I thought they had.

I swear to fall upon them all
And – what's that then?
(*He peers in backstage again.*)
Did I hear someone call?
ESMERALDA (*off*). My lord, my lord –
LUKE.

Aha, it is the voice of one I love.
I hear her through this rosy grove,
The lady whom I should have married.
Now they must know their plot's miscarried –
For she and I as man and wife
We shall pursue them all our mortal life
And never cease to –
(ESMERALDA *enters wearing* MERLIN'S *gown with the hood pulled over her head.*)
What is this –
Where is the face I used to kiss?
(*She holds her face well away from him, revealing to the audience that she is wearing a monstrous mask.*)
Your aspect is most sorely changed –
Tell me, my love, are you deranged?
ESMERALDA.

Not deranged – enchanted.
Alone in my chamber I was confronted
By so horrible an apparition
That I am scarcely in condition
To explain in simple syllables what took place:
But certain he did something dreadful to my face –
Do not look upon me! Or flesh, blood and bone,
Arms, legs and head, you will be turned to stone!
I know it past all question to be true
I tried it out just now on one or two
Old aunts and uncles in the garden
Who met my gaze and straight began to harden.
My face is all black magic and my hair

Has turned to serpents – oh true love – beware –
Each eye of mine is now a murderous organ:
I was your love but now I am a gorgon!
Kill me – kill me – Hocuss – hocus-pocus – I'm
  finished, carry on . . .

KING OF FRANCE. This English tragedy is almost too terrifying
to be endured. Such monstrosities upon the stage are scarcely
decent – but no matter – we will endeavour to accustom
ourselves to the horror of the scene. It is certainly well acted.

LUKE.
No. I will not kill you.
Such an idea is a counsel of despair.
It would be better to lock you up in this box lined
  with lead
And from the world conceal your dreadful head.
While you remain hid
We can drop your food and water through a slot in
  the lid.
In the meantime I will set afoot a thorough investi-
  gation
Find out this false enchanter who has wrought this
  transformation –
Find out the other murderers (or perhaps are they
  the same?)
Through whose poisonous plots my whole family has
  been slain,
And when I have discovered them –
When I have discovered them –
And when I have discovered them –
Oh, my God, I'm at a loss . . .

He has by now got ESMERALDA *shut in the box, and he ranges
the stage apparently in a frenzy but in fact searching for inspira-
tion. The* CONSTABLE *enters at the back of the audience – he is
suffering from delayed concussion, and carries a huge sword.*

CONSTABLE. Discovered them? Them? Discovered them, did you say?

LUKE (*trying to bring him into the play*). Discovered, yes, discovered.

CONSTABLE. I once believed that I could discover. Detect was the word that we used to employ.

LUKE. Detect – very good, that's exactly what I want.

CONSTABLE. Ah yes, but what? I mean, that's the question – what? (*Advancing on to the stage.*) I thought it was no more than a crown made of cardboard. The son of the King and I would have struck him with my truncheon! His father is the huge King and his crown is on his head and his head is made of cardboard and there is no doubt whatever that he will kill me when he sees me . . .

(*He suddenly fixes his eyes on the crown that* LUKE *is wearing.*)

Look, look he does see me – his wide glaring eyes cry out for revenge upon his son the injured Prince and his horn upon his forehead like the horn of a rhinoceros –

    Rhino rhino in your fury and your pride
    I will strike off your hard head
    With my great sword and wide –

LUKE (*holding him off with his player's sword*). Hey-up, no you don't –

CONSTABLE(*fighting* LUKE).

    He ducks below and I strike too high –
    Next time goes the point of it
    Right into his red eye.

LUKE. He swings too short and he swings too wide
    My death runs past on the left-hand side.

CONSTABLE.

    Down at his legs and cut them off
    By God and he jumps right over the top.
    Once again –

LUKE.

    And in vain –

CONSTABLE.
> I was under his chin.

LUKE. But he's gone and he's dodged –

LUKE runs backstage.

CONSTABLE.
> And he's run away in.

He follows after LUKE, whirling his sword. LUKE reappears and addresses the audience.

LUKE. I knew his ugly face as soon as he walked on. The question is – does he know mine? I doubt it. Is he drunk? Or is he running lunatic? That sword of his is real, which is more than can be said for mine – dear goodness, I never thought I'd be in for the like of this when I agreed to be an actor.
(*The* CONSTABLE *enters once again, sees* LUKE *and roars.*)
He's caught sight of me once again – I've got no alternative but to carry it through to the end – the show, as they say – has got to go on!
(*A great chase supervenes – at intervals, when he can,* LUKE *throws off a few remarks as though part of the play.*)
Thus my unfortunate kingdom, imperilled by lunatic conspirators – because there is no doubt in my mind that this is the very villain – he has destroyed all my family – thus my kingdom must await – in trepidation and helplessness – the inevitable duel to the death that you see enacted before you –

PRINCE (*to* LUKE). Keep going, keep going, you have him bewildered – confuse him – outwit him –
(*To the* PRINCESS.)
Of course it's the same man that we had our little trouble with. Very convenient – really – to have him dealt with in all the fury of a melodrama.

PRINCESS (*as* LUKE *and the* CONSTABLE *scramble all over the hall*). So elegant, so delightful, so athletic – the grace of these

English actors! Their virility – *Monseigneur*, is it not enchantment?

KING OF FRANCE. We are not at all clear as to precisely what is going on. But the performance, in all truth, is of a most singular dexterity.

The CONSTABLE *has now chased* LUKE *out of the hall altogether. He is left alone, very out of breath. He sits down upon the box.*

CONSTABLE.
 A breathing space.
 Here upon this box
 Take breath, wipe from my clotted locks
 The blood and sweat. Take stock. Shock?
 Being, as you see, terrible, in state of suspended shock . . .
 I chased him and I lost him
 And I found him again and chased him.
 And now at last has he gone?
 He was wearing a crown. Let me see. I do see.
 One, I see, two, no I don't, I see three –
They weren't there before. Or were they? Don't remember. Can he have split himself up like an earthworm and so hoped to evade me? He is given away though, by his glittering top-hamper. We will see then if these three will split themselves likewise . . .

He advances with his sword upon the PRINCESS, *who screams. There is real panic among the royalty.*

PRINCE. No, by George, this goes too far – you will offend the King, sir – oh, what's the good of talking to him – he's as mad as a hatter – where on earth is that man Luke?

LUKE (*entering from behind the audience*). It's all right. It's all off. It's all under control. The crown's off –
(*He has taken his own crown off.*)
I've put it down. Cardboard. It's all cardboard. They're all

three of them cardboard – so put them all down.

(*In some bewilderment, the royalty obey him. The* CONSTABLE *looks at him in a dazed manner.*)

All that you can see is cut out of cardboard and paper with nothing more dangerous than a little pair of scissors. Look, here they are . . .

(*He stands in front of the* CONSTABLE *and snips in the air with a pair of scissors, hypnotizing him. When the* CONSTABLE *appears to be fixed by the movement of the scissors,* LUKE *begins to sing.*)

'Cardboard and paper and patches and glue
Pleated and crumpled and folded in two
With a pair of white fingers and a little bit of skill
We make a whole world for the children to kill.
Prop them up on the table and set them in a row
And from the far corner lean your face out and blow
They'll all tumble down, both the sword and the
    crown
And the glittering gold weathercocks on the towers of
    the town.
After they've fallen the clouds will grow dark
And the children will creep home from the cold
    empty park
The raindrops will soak the wet cardboard into mud
Will soak the dark hair on your hot little head
Will soak the hard crust on your butterless bread
And the clothes on your back and the shoes where
    you tread –
Then the sheets on the bed
Then the leaves on the trees
Wetter than the warm wet westerly breeze –
So lie down, lie, lie and grow dry
Wrapped in a blanket and drowsy your eye.
Tomorrow you'll cry and tomorrow you can weep
All you need now is to fall fast asleep . . .'

There you are now, he's fixed, he's in a trance. And now: the opportunity to get him to undo all the mischief he has caused. Are you receiving me? Are you receiving me?

ESMERALDA (*in the box*). I am receiving you.

LUKE. Thank God for that . . . Loud and clear?

ESMERALDA. Loud and clear.

LUKE (*to* CONSTABLE). You are the false magician who turned my love into a gorgon.

CONSTABLE. Gorgon. Gorgon. Yes that's right. So I did. What's a gorgon?

LUKE. Those who behold the gorgon turn straightaway to stone.

CONSTABLE. Stone? Stone . . . ah, stone.

LUKE. You know it. Don't prevaricate. You are now willing, are you not, to remove the spell from her forthwith?

CONSTABLE. Forthwith.

LUKE. Then say it, after me. Arise, poor lady, from out your living tomb.

CONSTABLE. Arise, poor lady, from out your living tomb!

LUKE.

She does arise – she does –

(*He gives the box a kick and* ESMERALDA *slowly and painfully climbs out.*)

I hide my face for safety – woe alas.

CONSTABLE. Eh eh eh eh eh eh eh eh – gorgon – !

LUKE. Speak to her – release her –

CONSTABLE. She's turning me to stone!

LUKE. Oh no no, she can't be – you're not liable – you're the magician! Look sharp, now – can't you? She's not yet petrified your vocal chords – speak to her – tell her – 'you are once more a woman, free and beautiful'.

CONSTABLE. You are once more a woman, free – and – and –

ESMERALDA (*taking off the gorgon mask*). Well, free, at any rate.

LUKE. And beautiful.

ESMERALDA. Not very – I'm still suffering the after effects of the –

LUKE. Hocus-pocus, of course. You can't be expected to recover all at once. But in time, my love, you shall, my dearest love, you shall . . .

>Now at long last we join our married hands,
>A King and Queen in twin magnificence:
>While the false miscreant for ever stands
>A stone memorial to his own malevolence.
>Let all the little children run and leap
>And throw their eggs at him and throw their rotten tripe
>And caper round his base in mockery –
>We have concluded all his trickery.
>And so we kiss – and so we here embrace –
>And so our land is once again at peace!

(*The* PRINCE *gets up and joins them.*)

PRINCE.

>England at peace with France and all the world!
>How happy a resolution this to ancient sour discord.
>The gods will smile on you, and on you too,
>And on your marriage and your policy.
>We all congratulate you on your artistry –

And on your improvisation too – but what on earth has *he* to do with it?

This last remark, in an undertone, refers to the CONSTABLE *who is standing like a statue, tragic and rigid. There is general applause.*

LUKE. Oh, him – you might well ask.

KING OF FRANCE. Is it – is it finished?

PRINCE. I think so, *Monseigneur* . . . It is?

LUKE. It is.

The royal personages resume their crowns.

KING OF FRANCE. Indeed it was a play full of many surprises . . .

FRENCH OFFICER. There is, however, one question. Why, when the play is presented in the Court of the King of France, have you found it to be necessary to clothe your assassin in the uniform of one of our own officers?

LUKE. Yes, of course. Yes, that's right. In England, as it were, we're all anxious for peace. Right. But of course there's always those that claim that peace with the French can never be relied on. Warmongers is the word. Like, they apply it to the French. But we know, as you know, that this is not the case. Right?

FRENCH OFFICER. It is most certainly not the case.

LUKE. So: the man that makes the French out to be the biggest villains in the world is himself the biggest villain, and therefore we dress him up as a Frenchman so we pay him back in his own coin. Poetic justice, right – ? Very clever satire really – right – ? Do you see what I am driving at?

KING OF FRANCE. Oh, I think so. It is – intellectual! Yes. We are very pleased indeed by the enormous vigour of your work. *Monsieur* Crock, you have astonished us, you have enlightened us, you have most thoroughly entertained us! We are graciously delighted to award to you at once the one hundred guineas that we promised for this evening!
Monsieur le Capitaine, hand *Monsieur* Crock the purse.

LUKE *has taken off his mask.*

FRENCH OFFICER (*gives him the purse, then does a double-take*). But, *Monseigneur*, this is not *Monsieur* Crock.

KING OF FRANCE. Why no, no more it is! So Mr Crock himself did not play the leading part? Forgive me – who are *you*? I have seen your face before somewhere – but where – I do not know? You were not presented to me with the others of your actors?

LUKE. No sir; I was not.

KING OF FRANCE. But why not? This is – peculiar. There is but one, two, three – and only the young lady have I ever

met before. *Explication, explication, s'il vous plaît, une explication . . .?*

PRINCESS. *Monseigneur*, does it matter? You have seen their
performance, you have awarded them the prize –

Enter the CROKES *and* WILLIAM, *recovered.*

CROKE. Awarded us the prize : Oh Your Majesty, this is too
much!

FRENCH OFFICER. You will pardon us for thinking, sir, it is a
great deal too much. Why did you not perform your play
with the full strength of your company, for which reason His
Majesty has brought you here?

PRINCE. I think, in fairness to all, we should tell the King the
truth. Your Majesty, Mr Croke and his good lady and these
two other gentlemen, by very great ill-luck, at the very last
moment, were taken seriously ill. What you saw tonight was
not a rehearsed play, but an absolute improvisation, presented, I may safely say, with complete success, by the
intrepid Mr Luke, normally the Stage Manager, and the
equally intrepid Miss Esmeralda, actress.

KING OF FRANCE. But this is remarkable! You deserve to have
two prizes for such courage and resource. *Monsieur le
Capitaine* – another purse of gold at once for these brave
actors!

FRENCH OFFICER. Alas, *Monseigneur*, the Exchequer is a little
bit depleted by reason of the war – it is not possible, I fear,
to expend more money this season upon the arts.

KING OF FRANCE. But gentlemen, we would indeed have
given it if we could . . .

CROKE *and the other* ACTORS *all kiss the* KING'S *gracious
hand, kiss each other and generally rejoice.*

LUKE (*suddenly*). I'm going to tell him.

ESMERALDA. No, no, you can't do that – !

LUKE. Yes I am, I'm going to tell him. Sir!

KING OF FRANCE. *Monsieur*. Are we addressed?

LUKE. You are. Old Croke and his missus and the funny little
pansy there – nay and Esmeralda, too, but she only had a
mouthful – were deliberately poisoned!

KING OF FRANCE. *Mon Dieu!* But by whom? In our Palace!
Our English guests! Poisoned? Is this true?

ESMERALDA. Perfectly true.

KING OF FRANCE. Then the honour of France has been called
into question – and the honour of France must immediately
be redeemed. *Monsieur le Capitaine* – an investigation –
instantly – you will set it afoot this very moment, now, you
will spare no-one – you will –

LUKE. You don't need to investigate very far. We know well
who did it! Your own French actors did it.

KING OF FRANCE. *Madame* Zénobie? – you accuse *Madame*
Zénobie? But this – is not possible . . .

LUKE. Isn't it just . . .?

KING OF FRANCE. No . . . no . . . there has been here a
very great mistake . . . *Madame* Zénobie, in any case, has
been disgraced and will appear no more upon the Royal
Stage of Paris. It will not be necessary to persecute the poor
woman further. We do not wish to cause pain and suffering to
any artist . . . My dear Prince, just one moment . . .
(*He takes the* PRINCE *aside.*)
For the future of our international relations, this unfortunate
business must not be noised abroad, *comprenez-vous?* I
would not for the world have the peace treaty made invali-
date. So how then can we best prevent these actors from
talking about it?

PRINCE. Not difficult at all. Let me handle it. I think I know
the way . . . Now, Mr Croke, you do appreciate that even
if true, these allegations are unable to be proved and may in
fact be complete fantasy?

CROKE. It is possible, of course – but I really do think – sir –
that something should be done. My poor wife has been taken
exceedingly ill – and – er –

MRS CROKE. Never in all my life have I experienced so much
pain. And before an audience too – the humiliation – the
indignity –

PRINCE. I am sure we all sympathize very deeply, Mrs Croke.
But let us not – er – let us not look solely upon the dark side
of the affair. Suppose now that my father – and I am sure
that he will – were to offer you – all of you – a permanent
contract as players to the Royal Household? We have no
company of actors at present in receipt of regular salaries
from the Crown, and I for one, have, regretted this, for a
long time. The King of France has his own theatre – why
should not the King of England? What do you say to that –
well, what do you say to it, Mrs Croke?

MRS CROKE. Oh, Your Royal Highness –

CROKE. I am overwhelmed –

PRINCE. Exactly so. So – no more trouble? And of course you
have the hundred guineas?

LUKE. Oh no sir – pardon me. *I* have the hundred guineas.
It was no chance that I did not consume
Your poisoned dinner in this very room.
I was regarded as being by far too rough:
I had to buckle-to and work while you sat down to
stuff.
But she stood up and she walked forth,
This very day, you saved their play:
And now you share the prize.
Therefore if you're willing, we will say our fond
good-byes.
Take yourselves off to London, act before the King:
We two will attempt together a far more dangerous
thing.
We will travel, hand in hand,
Across water and dry land –
We will entertain the people
Under castle-wall and proud church steeple

Throughout Switzerland and Germany
And the arid plains of Spain –
You're going to get a nice fat subsidy –
You can leave with us your scenery,
You'll not need that again.
In any case, by my workmanship it came to its present
    state,
So I fancy if I claim it there can be no just dispute.

He and ESMERALDA *fold up the scenery and begin to carry it off.*

WILLIAM. Wait one moment – no – you cannot possibly –

PRINCE. Oh I think they can, sir – yes – I really think it's better this way. Don't you think so, Mr Croke? Mrs Croke? No?

MRS CROKE. I have no intention whatever of expending words upon such unprofessional ingratitude.

CROKE. Oh never mind them, never mind them, my dear –
    (*He sings.*)
    'We're all going to London
    And our bonnets are a-cock
    Dirty grouchy grumblers
    Need not share in our good luck –
    The King is now our patron
    And the Prince will wish us well
    And those who do not like it
    They can rapidly run to hell!'

The CROKES *and* WILLIAM *go out singing and dancing.*

PRINCESS. Permit me for one moment to wish *you* well, *Monsieur* Luke – and Esmeralda – perhaps, before too long, we shall see you act again – in England?

KING OF FRANCE. But certainly not in France. You are to leave this country at once, sir: and never never never return to it again. *Monsieur le Capitaine* – you will make certain that he takes his immediate departure.

The royalty are about to go out when the KING *suddenly becomes aware of the* CONSTABLE – *still standing like a statue.*

Oh yes – I was intending to ask. In God's name – who is this?

LUKE. Oh, he's all right. He's a statue. He'll decorate your Palace for you. And if he don't – he'll wander home again. Nobody's worried about *him* any more. Are we right then? Let's get moving.

He and ESMERALDA *go out one side.*
The ROYALS *go out the other.*
After a pause the CONSTABLE *slowly comes to life and starts to sing.*

CONSTABLE (*sings*).

    'I do not know what has been happening
    I do not know where I am now
    I wish I had a little farmyard
    With a pair of chickens and a cow.
    It is no use to be a policeman
    The force of anarchy wins all the time:
    I did not like what I saw around me
    I did not like it so I called it crime.
    With a truncheon and a brace of handcuffs
    I did my best for Order and Law:
    I was overwhelmed by such loose behaviour
    Such goings-on I never saw.
    And now the Kings have stuck their foot in
    And made it legal what was not allowed.
    There's nothing more for me to do – sirs –
    But to hide away from the madding crowd.
    I will become a hairy hermit
    And live alone in a scruffy old cell:
    I never felt such a fool before – sirs –
    I suppose you'll say: it's just as well.'

He staggers stiffly out.

Methuen's Modern Plays

EDITED BY JOHN CULLEN AND GEOFFREY STRACHAN

Simon Gray	*Spoiled*
	Butley
Peter Handke	*Offending the Audience and*
	Self-Accusation
	Kaspar
	The Ride Across Lake Constance
Rolf Hochhuth	*The Representative*
Heinar Kipphardt	*In the Matter of J. Robert Oppenhei*
Arthur Kopit	*Chamber Music and other plays*
	Indians
Jakov Lind	*The Silver Foxes Are Dead*
	and other plays
David Mercer	*On the Eve of Publication*
	After Haggerty
	Flint
	The Bankrupt and other plays
	Duck Song
John Mortimer	*The Judge*
	Five Plays
	Come As You Are
	A Voyage Round My Father
	Collaborators
Joe Orton	*Crimes Of Passion*
	Loot
	What the Butler Saw
	Funeral Games and The Good and
	Faithful Servant
	Entertaining Mr Sloane
Harold Pinter	*The Birthday Party*
	The Room and the Dumb Waiter
	The Caretaker
	A Slight Ache and other plays
	The Collection and The Lover
	The Homecoming
	Tea Party and other plays
	Landscape and Silence
	Old Times
David Selbourne	*The Damned*
Jean-Paul Sartre	*Crime Passionnel*
Wole Soyinka	*Madmen and Specialists*
	The Jero Plays
Boris Vian	*The Empire Builders*
Peter Weiss	*Trotsky in Exile*
Theatre Workshop	*Oh What a Lovely War*
and Charles Chilton	
Charles Wood	*'H'*
	Veterans
Carl Zuckmayer	*The Captain of Köpenick*

*   *   *

Methuen Playscripts

Michael Abbensetts	*Sweet Talk*
Paul Ableman	*Tests*
	Blue Comedy